SO-CAP-798

Wonders in the Midst

by Ward Patterson

cover art by Greg LaFever

"And I will stretch out my hand, and smite Egypt with all my wonders which I will do in the midst thereof: and after that he will let you go" (Exodus 3:20, KJV).

You may obtain a 64-page leader's guide to accompany this paperback. Order number 40077 from Standard Publishing or your local supplier.

A Division of Standard Publishing
Cincinnati, Ohio 45231
No. 40076

© 1979, The STANDARD PUBLISHING Company, a division of STANDEX INTERNATIONAL Corporation.

Library of Congress Catalog No. 78-62709

ISBN: 0-87239-237-6

Printed in U.S.A.   1979

Contents

Introduction
The Wonder of God's Ways

"Thou art the God who workest wonders; Thou hast made known Thy strength among the peoples" (Psalm 77:14).

The Scriptures are a revelation of the wonderful works of God. The psalmist wrote, "He has made His wonders to be remembered; The Lord is gracious and compassionate" (Psalm 111:4).

The birth of the nation of Israel was marked by an outpouring of God's gracious and compassionate wonders. Beginning with the miraculous deliverance from captivity in Egypt, continuing through the years of wilderness instruction in the ways and will of God, culminating in the conquest of the promised land, God's wonders protected, saved, directed, corrected, led, and sustained His people.

To recount all of God's wonderful acts during this formative period in Israel's history would be impossible. We feel the same frustration as the psalmist who wrote, "Many, O Lord my God, are the wonders which Thou hast done, and Thy thoughts toward us; there is none to compare with Thee; if I would declare and speak of them, they would be too numerous to count" (Psalm 40:5). We see them everywhere in the history of God's dealings with Israel.

5

The wonders of God were purposeful. They accomplished specific and immediate ends. They freed slaves, they eliminated enemies, they destroyed cities, they punished wickedness. They were also rhetorical. They were intended to convey a message not only to the Israelites but to all people to follow. Included in that message were the truths that God is all powerful, that He is jealous for His name and reputation, that He is concerned about inequity and iniquity, that He is loving and righteous, and that He punishes and rewards.

These wonders of God were to be pondered and taught. They were to be remembered and recounted as keys into understanding the ways of God. Providing instruction for the young and encouragement for the weak, they continued to live and bring hope and direction to all subsequent generations.

The wonders of God were miracles to be treasured as the heritage of a people uniquely singled out to witness the power and love of God revealed in history. They were monuments of remembrance to be burned into the consciousness of His people in such a way that those people would ever bear the brand of the one true God. They were marvels to excite the mind with the message of God's longsuffering and lovingkindness despite the frailties of sinful man.

In the pages to follow we will seek God's wonderful lessons to the present as we journey with Israel toward the promised land.

1

The Wonder of God's Provision

(Moses and the Princess)

Text: Exodus 2:1-10
Suggested Reading: Exodus 1, 2; Acts 7:17-22

"Remember His wonderful deeds which He has done, His marvels and the judgments from His mouth . . ." (1 Chronicles 16:12).

A population explosion was going on in Egypt, and Pharaoh was not pleased (Acts 7:17). On the surface of things, Pharaoh ought to have been delighted with reports from his court scribes and statisticians of the fruitfulness of his captives. After all, those descendants of Jacob and his children who immigrated during the time of Vizier Joseph were a fine assist to the gross national product of the land of the Nile. They were an excellent source of cheap labor and, as such, were a fine natural resource.

Pharaoh's Problem

There was, however, one problem that plagued Pharaoh. The Israelites, only seventy in number when they arrived nearly four hundred years before, now numbered over two million. That large population, Pharaoh felt, might in fact be a time-bomb ticking in the midst of Egypt. He and his military advisors talked of a war scenario: enemy attack from without, Israelite revolt from within. It did not sound at all good.

7

Pharaoh's Plan

So Pharaoh instituted a rather harsh program of birth control, to be applied to those highly fertile Israelite subjects (Exodus 1:10, 11). First the plan was to work them to death. Exhausted, ill-treated, harassed, beaten down, discouraged, battered people, so the theory went, would not have interest or desire to bring children into their dreadful world. But overwork and bitter, hard bondage didn't lower the birth rate. If anything it only increased it (Exodus 1:12).

So the king of Egypt decided to take more direct and drastic action. He, of course, wanted to preserve the compliant work force as much as possible while at the same time diminishing the possibility of revolt. He felt that he could accomplish this best by decreeing the death of all the male babies.

We can imagine how the news of the pharaonic policy was received by the people of Israel. Pharaoh was, by his policies, creating exactly what he feared—a rebellious, bitter, vengeful segment likely to choose any means that offered deliverance from his brutality.

Pharaoh attempted to enforce his plan through control of the obstetricians of the day—the chief midwives. This is where his plan broke down. The Hebrew midwives, despite whatever fear they had of the heartless ruler, were not about to do what he commanded (Exodus 1:17). Their loyalty was to God. They proceeded with business as usual in the work camps of the Hebrews.

Pharaoh, who had a way of keeping his eye on such things, kept getting reports of men children appearing in the homes of the slaves. When the midwives were called to account, they put out a cover story. They said that because Hebrew women gave birth quickly they never arrived in time to carry out the king's edict before the baby was hidden. Their story was sufficiently plausible to enable them to escape punishment. And

8

the God-fearing midwives prospered in the midst of the persecuted community. Pharaoh, not to be thwarted, applied pressure to the parents themselves, commanding that they drown their sons in the rivers and canals of Egypt (Exodus 1:22).

A pregnancy is a special time for a family as it looks forward to the birth of the child. Given the situation in Egypt at that time, however, it must have been a time of great anxiety for an expectant Hebrew parent. Such must have been the case with Amram and Jochebed, the father and mother of the beautiful little baby who would come to be known as Moses.

For three months his mother nursed and hid her little son. But as the child grew and his cries in the night became more difficult to stifle, she sorrowfully came to the point where she knew that she could keep him no longer.

The king's edict had been that every baby boy must be cast into the river (Exodus 1:22). She complied with the letter of this edict, if not with its evil spirit. She cast her three month old baby into the river—but she provided a special mummy-like wrapping. She took papyrus reeds and bound them together into a little boat similar to those commonly used in the marshes by fishermen. She covered the reeds with pitch to hold the water away from his little body.

His mother floated the little bundle of papyrus and pitch out into the current of the river—and right into Pharaoh's very palace.

Pharaoh's Princess

What a remarkable voyage that little boy took! It just so happened that Pharaoh's daughter and her attendants were along the river's bank just as that little bundle of baby bobbed by. She was curious as to what that floating thing might be, so she sent one of her attendants splashing out into the water after it.

Sound came from the reed and pitch parcel as the attendant laid it before the princess. When the little boat was opened, the muffled cries of the kicking, squirming child became louder. He was irresistible. The princess fell in love with that squalling, round-faced little Hebrew child with chubby hands reaching out to take hold of her finger.

It must have been about then that Miriam, the baby's sister, finally began to breathe again. She had watched the little bundle as her mother set it adrift. And while he's mother returned home, too sorrowful to watch what happened to the little boat, the baby's sister had followed its drifting with curious eyes.

What were her feelings as she saw the Egyptian women take the bundle from the water and open it? Did she expect these Egyptians to drown this baby just for the fun of it? Did she think about running into their midst and snatching the baby from them? Or did she pray to God as she had never prayed before?

When she saw the response of the Egyptian princess to her baby brother she moved resolutely, and perhaps fearfully, toward those Egyptian court beauties. She offered her help to the princess—her help to find someone from among the Hebrews to nurse the baby.

God's Providence

Why was this high-born lady so quick to take the little girl's suggestion? She had decided to keep the baby, at least for a time. Since he was Hebrew it probably would have been risky to seek help among the Egyptians who might report her to her father. A Hebrew nurse was the obvious answer. She probably could have worked that out herself, but the little girl's suggestion offered the least possibility of exposure. And of course the marvelous providence of God was at work in it all.

When the princess told her to go and do as she had suggested, little Miriam must have run with all the strength and excitement of her young years. It was too good to be believed. "Mother! Come quickly! We have a chance to save his life!"

Jochebed must have come fearfully to the place where the princess sat along the river bank, smiling into the face of that little drifter, nuzzling him and making him laugh. One false step . . . one wrongly spoken word . . .

But somehow, despite the hazards, it all worked out. The princess told the baby's real mother to take care of the child. She even provided the funds for his keep. She continued to look out for him as he grew older. Eventually he came to live, as her son, in Pharaoh's own household. She called him Moses, a name suggested to her from the fact that she had taken him out of the water.

What a remarkable story of God's wonderful ways! God was preparing a very special person for leadership among His people. He was a man of two worlds, conscious of his Hebrew heritage through the teachings of his mother, sophisticated in the learning of the Egyptians through the provision of his foster mother. He would be a gifted man, highly educated with the best training to be afforded in the court of the king of Egypt. He would be a compassionate man, touched by the suffering of his enslaved people.

Who was the hero of these events? Moses, of course, emerges as the center of attention. But what of that extraordinary little girl who could not bear to abandon her little brother to the unknown? Quickwitted and bold, she, more than anyone else, intervened at the critical point to turn an uncertain situation to good. Then, of course, there was Pharaoh's daughter who, in her independence, rose above racial hatred to love a child she was supposed to despise. And how about Moses' parents? Hebrews 11:23 notes that they demonstrated faithfulness to God in their resistance to the king's edict. But the real hero, finally, was God. In His special, extraordinary way, He brought victory in circumstances that promised only defeat.

God works His wonders in and through people. Moses will be the center of our attention in several chapters that follow, but it must be remembered that he could never have accomplished what he did if it had not been for some lesser-known people of faith who did what they could in the face of uncertainty and defeat.

When God chose to do a mighty work, a wonder in the midst of Israel, He first prepared a person. He provided life, He provided deliverance, He provided nurture. He continues, in our day, to work wonders through those to whom He gives life, deliverance, and sustenance.

Timeless Truths

• It is often in our greatest desperation and weakness that we see God's providence most clearly.

• To place a Hebrew in the court of the king would have been impossible for men, but God put a special baby there with no difficulty at all. We should not doubt the ingenuity of God's ways. He can arrange things that seem impossible to us.

2

The Wonder of God's Call

(Moses and the Burning Bush)

Text: Exodus 3, 4
Suggested Reading: Exodus 2:11—4:31;
Acts 7:22-36; Hebrews 11:23-26

"And when Moses saw it, he began to marvel at the sight . . ."
(Acts 7:31).

What was it like for Moses to grow up a man of two worlds? What interest in his education and growth did his Egyptian foster mother take? What did he learn of the technology and mythology of Egypt? How did he assimilate the culture around him? What language did he learn? How was he accepted by the Egyptians, and Pharaoh in particular? And how did he feel when he saw the ill treatment of his people by those who treated him well? Was he ever fearful, ashamed, resentful, or confused about the peculiar circumstances that God had put him in? Did his real mother suggest to him that he might be a child of destiny, chosen by God to be an instrument of deliverance?

We can only guess at the answers to these questions, for the Bible does not choose to reveal them to us. Rather, the narrative jumps from his early youth to a dramatic event that took place nearly forty years later.

Moses, from all appearances, was still enjoying favor in pharaonic circles. Yet his heart was with the people of his birth who suffered under the yoke of Egypt. He was now a mature man and perhaps he was in the process of making the fateful choice that marked him as one of the greats of the faith (Hebrews 11:24-26).

Significant Choice

He might have chosen to insulate himself from the world of the captive Hebrews, but he did not. He went among them. A vision of their deliverance formed in his mind's eye. And he was the obvious person to bring that about (Acts 7:25).

The time had come for positive action, so Moses thought. No longer could he look the other way and ignore the brutality his true people suffered daily. When he saw an Egyptian viciously beating a Hebrew, he took a decisive action from which he could never turn back. Using skills he probably learned in Pharaoh's court, he struck down the Egyptian, then disposed of the body, burying it in the sand.

We are not told clearly the thoughts and emotions that moved Moses to this act. Did he act on impulse, or was he taking a conscious step toward the deliverance of his oppressed people? Stephen indicated that it was probably the latter (Acts 7:24, 25).

News of Moses' deed spread throughout the Hebrew people in the campfire whispers of the night. Were the whispers set in motion by the Hebrew whose cause Moses had taken? Or was the murder observed by someone unknown to Moses? Was it known only by one or two? Or was this murder of the Egyptian widely known throughout the Hebrew camp? If so, was there debate about its meaning for the future of the Hebrew nation? Were the people aware of Moses' life and resentful of his preferred treatment while they suffered? Or was there hope that God was raising up a leader for them to follow out of bondage?

14

Whatever the case, Moses went out among the Hebrews the following day unaware that his own life was in jeopardy. Moses was used to deference and the power that his unique position brought him. When he saw two Hebrews fighting, he stepped in to play the role of peacemaker and arbiter. The offender did not strike him with his fists as he had been striking his companion. Rather he struck him with his mouth, with words that must have taken Moses' breath away: "Who made you a prince or a judge over us? Are you intending to kill me, as you killed the Egyptian?" (Exodus 2:14).

Shattered Vision

Moses' vision of leadership among the Hebrews was shattered. If this man knew, then many others probably knew. And if the Hebrews knew, it would not be long till Pharaoh knew. It was time for haste. Moses moved as quickly as he could. Saying good-bye to the "good life" he had known since his youth, he became a fugitive. He was on Pharaoh's most-wanted list (Exodus 2:15) as he eluded border garrisons and fled toward the east, into the wilderness of Midian.

In Midian Moses entered another period of learning. Far from the pomp and power of Pharaoh, Moses learned the lessons of solitude, reflection, and quiet. He joined himself to the clan of Jethro, a shepherd. He married one of Jethro's daughters, Zipporah, and had sons.

Spiritual Preparation

What went through Moses' mind during the long hours he sat on the hillsides of Midian? As the flock followed him to the watering places, faithfully depending on his providence and leadership, did his mind ever visualize the flock as a great company of people following him to freedom? Did his vision remain strong and passionate? Or did it die in the humiliation of his disgrace and rejection in Egypt? For forty years Moses learned patience and humility.

On the surface, it might seem that these were wasted years, but not so. They were a part of God's plan for deliverance. God had not forgotten His people (Exodus 2:23-25).

Sinaitic Call

One day when Moses was moving his flock near the mountain called Horeb or Sinai, his attention was drawn by a peculiar sight. There was a fire. As he moved closer to it, he noticed that while the bush burned with great flame and heat, the bush itself was not being consumed. His curiosity aroused, Moses went closer.

Suddenly he heard a mighty voice calling his name. He was told to remove his sandals, for he was standing on holy ground. The voice said, "I am the God of your father, the God of Abraham, the God of Isaac, and the God of Jacob" (Exodus 3:6). God noted His concern for the oppression of Israel and His desire to bring them into "a land flowing with milk and honey" (Exodus 3:7-9).

This was all well and good, from Moses' point of view. But then God said, "I will send *you* to Pharaoh, so that *you* may bring My people, the sons of Israel, out of Egypt" (Exodus 3:10). Moses was not sure he really wanted to become involved. He had tried something like that before, and it had been a dismal failure. He might still be on the most-wanted list in Egypt. And he knew how the Egyptians felt about letting the Hebrews leave.

He knew it would be hard for anyone to establish himself as a leader of Israel. He knew the Hebrews would question his credentials. God told him to say to them, "I AM has sent me to you" (Exodus 3:14).

Yahweh, God, gave him specific instructions as to what he should say. "Go and gather the elders of Israel together, and say to them, 'The Lord, the God of your fathers, the God of Abraham, Isaac and Jacob, has appeared to me, saying, "I am indeed concerned about you and what has been done to you in Egypt" ' " (Exodus 3:16). God further promised that this time the Israelites would pay attention to him. And though Pharaoh would resist, God would do great wonders in the midst of Egypt and bring about the promised deliverance.

Startling Signs

Still Moses doubted that the Hebrews would receive him as sent from God. God therefore gave him three signs that would demonstrate God's presence with him. His staff, when thrown on the ground, would become a snake. And when he took hold of it again, it would again become a staff. If he put his hand into his cloak, it would be leprous when removed again. And if he put this leprous hand into his cloak, it would be normal when removed. If he took water from the Nile and poured it out on the dry ground, it would become blood (Exodus 4:1-9).

God surely was supplying Moses with wonders to do in the midst of Egypt. But what about Moses himself? Moses was unsure of his speaking and leading abilities. He protested that he was not eloquent and that he was thus not properly equipped by nature to be God's messenger. God replied, "Now then go, and I, even I, will be with your mouth, and teach you what you are to say" (Exodus 4:12).

When Moses still protested, suggesting that God really ought to send someone else, God was angry with him (Exodus 4:13, 14). Aaron, his elder brother, would be his spokesman. God said, "And you are to speak to him and put the words in his mouth; and I, even I, will be with your mouth and his mouth, and I will teach you what you are to do" (Exodus 4:15).

So Moses and his family began a journey into the unknown. They returned to Egypt, equipped with God's power, His wonders, and His signs. Moses was now eighty years old, and there lay ahead of him a formidable task.

Moses' confrontation with the eternal, self-existent, absolute God at Sinai and his call to service in His name was a turning point in his life. The Christian, like Moses, is a called one. The acceptance of God's call marks a turning point in the life of the believer. Peter wrote, "As obedient children, do not be conformed to the former lusts which were yours in your ignorance, but like the Holy One who called you, be holy yourselves also in all your behavior . . ." (1 Peter 1:14, 15). To be called is to be set apart to God's holy work in our lives. Paul wrote to the Thessalonians, "But we should always give thanks to God for you, brethren beloved by the Lord, because God has chosen you from the beginning for salvation through sanctification by the Spirit and faith in the truth. And it was for this He called you through our gospel, that you may gain the glory of our Lord Jesus Christ" (2 Thessalonians 2:13, 14).

We feel somehow very closely akin to Moses as he reasoned with God about his limitations. He had tried to be a deliverer and had been rejected. He was keenly aware of the difficulties that lay ahead and he needed to be reminded of the strength that God would provide. He was a realist whom God was going to transform into a visionary.

Timeless Truths

• When we try to take things into our own hands and do God's work in our own strength, we are very likely to fail.

- God often brings us an awareness of weakness and failure before He brings us success. The best preparation for handling success may be the experiencing of failure.
- On the surface of it, the time in Midian seemed wasted, but in God's school for Moses it was an important learning period. Quiet and contemplation are as necessary to greatness as are education and training.
- Moses learned the geography of Midian as a shepherd. This knowledge would be useful when he entered that region with the large nation of the Hebrews. Lowly tasks prepare us for big ones.
- When God calls us to His task He provides what is necessary for us to perform that task.
- Moses had eighty years of preparation for forty years of leadership.
- Heart and soul training are as important to God's leaders as are ability and education.
- "What then shall we say to these things? If God is for us, who is against us?" (Romans 8:31).

3

The Wonder of God's Deliverance

(Moses and the Plagues)

Text: Exodus 6:1-13; 11:1-10; 14:21-31
Suggested Reading: Exodus 5:1—15:21;
Hebrews 11:27-29

"He sent signs and wonders into your midst, O Egypt, upon Pharaoh and all his servants" (Psalm 135:9). "And He brought forth His people with joy, His chosen ones with a joyful shout" (Psalm 105:43).

The stage was set for one of the greatest confrontations of all history. On the one side was God's man, Moses, the eighty-year-old prince/shepherd/prophet, equipped with a call from God, a simple staff, and an eighty-three-year-old brother. On the other side was the mighty king of one of the world's great empires, a man who could summon six hundred chariots with one word and who held power of life and death over millions of subject Hebrews. It was a confrontation that demonstrated to Egyptians and to Hebrews alike that there was no god like unto Jehovah. The wonders He was to do in their midst would burn themselves into the consciousnesses of the children of Israel for all time. They learned that it was not by their power that they could escape Egypt, but by the unlimited power and provision of the one true God.

Return

What was in Moses' mind as he crossed again the border of the land of his youth? He knew that those who had sought his life were now dead (Exodus 4:19), but there must still have been some apprehension as he retraced the route he had taken in fear so many years before.

Wasting no time, he and Aaron went immediately to Pharaoh. "Thus says the Lord, the God of Israel, 'Let my people go that they may celebrate a feast to Me in the wilderness' " (Exodus 5:1). The haughty king replied with obvious contempt, "Who is the Lord that I should obey His voice to let Israel go?" (Exodus 5:2). He was soon to find out, much to the sorrow of the land of Egypt.

Rigor

Not only did Pharaoh deny Moses' request, but he also moved to make the Hebrews' life more exhausting than it already had been. He said the request of Moses was made because the people had too much time on their hands. So he gave command that the straw that formerly had been supplied to those making bricks would now have to be gathered by the workmen themselves. Though this took the Hebrews longer, the daily quotas were not diminished. Though they worked longer and harder than ever, they never could satisfy their taskmasters.

The Hebrew foremen presented their difficulties to Pharaoh, but he gave them no sympathy. Evidently he was trying to turn them against Moses and Aaron. If that was his goal he certainly was accomplishing it (Exodus 5:20, 21).

Moses' vision of service to his people was being tested. He prayed to God in discouragement, "O Lord, why hast Thou brought harm to this people? Why didst Thou ever send me? Ever since I came to Pharaoh to speak in Thy name, he has done harm to this people; and Thou hast not delivered Thy people at all" (Exodus 5:22, 23).

God's reply to Moses' prayer was a great affirmation of His love and concern for His oppressed people (Exodus 6:1-8). But when Moses attempted to share God's assurances with the Hebrews, they would not listen, so deep was their despair (Exodus 6:9).

Refusal

Moses wondered how he could get the king of Egypt to pay attention to him when his own people did not. Still, at the urging of God, Moses and Aaron once again stood before Pharaoh. There Moses demonstrated one of his wonders. He threw his staff to the ground. It became a serpent. Pharaoh, however, reacted only by calling in his magicians to do a similar feat. Their snakes were swallowed up by Moses' snake, and yet the king felt that his power had been vindicated over that of this God of Moses.

There followed a series of confrontations between the stubborn and forgetful king and the men of God, each round demonstrating the power of Jehovah over nature.

First the Nile was turned to blood so that the fish of the Nile died, the water stank, and it could no longer be used for drinking. The Egyptians were able to get drinking water only by digging down beside the rivers and canals for water filtered through the ground.

Then came the frogs, swarming up from the waters into the bedrooms and kitchens of the Egyptians. These wet, slimy creatures covered the land, squashing underfoot, hopping on the table, croaking loudly in the night.

Then came biting gnats. The magicians of Egypt had succeeded in imitating, somehow, the turning of water into blood and they succeeded in producing some frogs, but when it came to gnats they came up empty handed. Though they confessed to Pharaoh, "This is the finger of God," he nevertheless persisted

22

in resisting the will of God. His pattern was to promise to let the children of Israel go in order to get rid of the plague, then to reverse himself when the plague had been removed.

After the biting gnats came swarming insects, probably blood-sucking flies. Now the sound of buzzing flies filled the land, and the painful biting of gnats was replaced by the swarming persistence of flies. This plague, miraculously, touched only the Egyptians, not the Israelites (Exodus 8:22, 23).

Though he was still unwilling to grant what Moses asked, Pharaoh offered a compromise. He would allow them to sacrifice, but they would have to do it within the borders of Egypt (Exodus 8:25). Moses refused, noting that the sacrifice of sheep was objectionable to the Egyptians and that God had commanded them to go three days' journey into the wilderness.

Next came a severe pestilence among the animals of the Egyptians. Like some before it, this plague was clearly announced beforehand. Up until this time the plagues had been irritating and painful, but now, for the first time, a large loss of personal property was involved. The livestock in the fields of the Egyptians died, but that of the Hebrews was spared.

Then Moses, standing before Pharaoh, tossed ashes from a brickkiln into the sky, where the ashes became dust that spread over the land of Egypt and produced painful boils in both the Egyptians and their animals. The magicians, having already despaired of matching the wonders of Jehovah, had such painful boils that they could no longer attend the meetings of Moses and Pharaoh (Exodus 9:11).

Next came hail and rain, lightning and thunder, so terrible that those who were caught out in it were in danger of being pelted to death. Though this violent storm wrought havoc among the Egyptians, the Hebrews were once again spared. Pharaoh finally seemed to be coming to his senses. He confessed, "I have sinned this time; the Lord is the righteous one, and I and my people are the wicked ones. Make supplication to the Lord, for there has been enough of God's thunder and hail; and I will let you go, and you shall stay no longer" (Exodus 9:27, 28). True to form, however, he refused to let them depart once the plague was removed.

When Moses promised that locusts would be the next wonder God would perform in their midst, the Egyptians entreated Pharaoh to let the Hebrew men without their families go to worship as they requested. Pharaoh offered this compromise, knowing that keeping the women and children would assure their return. But when Moses rejected this compromise, Pharaoh once again returned to his adamant refusal.

The locusts came in with an east wind. Millions of those little creatures, which weigh only a few grams but eat their weight daily, devoured every living plant in their path. (One square mile of a swarm can contain as many as 200,000,000 insects, and swarms covering four hundred square miles have been recorded by researchers. Depending on wind conditions, a swarm can move from a few miles to sixty miles a day.) Already the crops of Egypt had been severely damaged by hail. The locusts signaled the absolute end of productive farming in the land. It is not surprising that this time Moses and Aaron were called in haste by Pharaoh, who blurted out, "I have sinned against the Lord your God and against you. Now therefore, please forgive my sin only this once, and make supplication to the Lord your God, that He would only remove this death from me" (Exodus 10:16, 17).

Yet when a west wind, at Moses' prayer, removed the locusts, Pharaoh once again reneged. Then came darkness, a great darkness that engulfed the land and shut out sunshine for three days. Pharaoh offered another compromise, suggesting that he would allow the Hebrews to go if they would leave behind their flocks and livestock. When this was rejected by Moses, Pharaoh said to him, "Get away from me! Beware, do not see my face again, for in the day you see my face you shall die!" (Exodus 10:28).

The final blow to Pharaoh's pride came with the death of the firstborn of man and beast among the Egyptians. The Hebrews were instructed to slay an unblemished lamb a year old and sprinkle its blood on the doorposts and lintels of their houses. The lamb was to be roasted and eaten with unleavened bread and bitter herbs, and the Hebrews were to eat it in haste, their clothing ready for travel (Exodus 12:11). God, at long last, with a mighty hand was going to lead them from Pharaoh's grip. That night, at midnight, the destroyer struck down all the firstborn of those houses where the blood was not on the door. Pharaoh arose to the cries of death in the night and at last, now with an urgency of deep fear and sorrow, he entreated the Hebrews to be gone lest all the Egyptians should die (Exodus 12:31-33).

Release

The Egyptians gave the Hebrews silver and gold and clothing and other precious things and sent them on their way. It had been a long confrontation—perhaps a year. But it was now over, and God had demonstrated His power to Egyptian and Israelite alike. There could be no questioning the fact that He was God of all and that He had chosen these descendants of Abraham as a means of exalting His name among the nations.

The final plague was never to be forgotten by the Hebrews. Their escape from death is still remembered in the Passover feast that is held annually. The Jewish calendar was reoriented to begin with the month of deliverance (Exodus 12:1, 2). Special instructions were given for the perpetual remembrance of the mighty way God had rescued His people. And with the birth of each firstborn, the nation was to be reminded of God's deliverance (Exodus 13:11-16).

The Christian sees vestiges of the Passover night in the Communion service. Jesus took the unleavened bread of that feast and the fruit of the vine and gave them holy significance as He identified them with His body and His blood shed for the sins of the world. As the blood of the lamb saved the Hebrews from destruction on that fateful night in Egypt, Jesus' shed blood protects His people from eternal destruction. Paul used the ceremonies of the Passover as a background for his urging to consecrated life, noting, "For Christ our Passover also has been sacrificed" (1 Corinthians 5:7).

It must have been a grand sight, those two and a half million people walking toward freedom. At the head of their columns went a pillar of cloud by day and a pillar of fire by night (Exodus 13:21, 22). If they noticed anything special about the direction God was leading them, they scarcely had time to think about it.

Rescue

Suddenly they found themselves in danger. Pharaoh had changed his mind and had hurriedly assembled a mobile force composed of his six hundred select chariots and all the others he could call up quickly. The camp of Moses was by the Red Sea, near Pihahiroth, and it seemed boxed in by the mountains and the sea. It looked as if the Hebrews' hope of freedom was to be snatched from them after all, at the very moment when they were about to breathe free at last. While some of the people cowered in fear, Moses shouted out, "Do not fear! Stand by and see the salvation of the Lord . . ." (Exodus 14:13).

Throughout the night the Hebrews were protected by the pillar of fire. Then God parted the sea before them so that they crossed over on dry land, the waters standing up like a wall on each side of them. When the Egyptians attempted to follow them, suddenly they found themselves having difficulty controlling their horses and chariots. Recognizing that something was amiss, they tried to flee. But it was too late. At the command of God, Moses stretched forth his hand over the sea; and the waters closed in to drown the pursuing army. With this final wonder of deliverance, Israel was free.

The account notes, "And when Israel saw the great power which the Lord had used against the Egyptians, the people feared the Lord, and they believed in the Lord and in His servant Moses" (Exodus 14:31). And Moses sang a great song of praise to Jehovah (Exodus 15:1-18). Among the lines of that great psalm were these: "Who is like Thee among the gods, O Lord? Who is like Thee, majestic in holiness, awesome in praises, working wonders?" (Exodus 15:11).

Timeless Truths

• God's name will be vindicated. Those who resist His will do it at their own peril.

• Moses and his people were specially set apart by God in their passing through the Red Sea. It was, as it were, a symbolic initiation into dependence on God. The water like a wall beside them by the power of God, the cloud over them and directing them—these typified their unity in God and their common salvation. Paul spoke of this as being "baptized into Moses in the cloud and in the sea" (1 Corinthians 10:2).

• The Passover lamb was to be unblemished, and no bone of it was to be broken. These simple stipulations span the years to Golgotha where Jesus hung on a cross. A soldier there pierced His side with a spear, though he had intended to break Christ's legs. John wrote, "For these things came to pass, that the Scripture might be fulfilled, 'Not a bone of Him shall be broken' " (John 19:36).

• God does not always take the swift and easy way when He wants to bring glory to His name.

• That which God begins He will finish. That which He promises will come to pass.

• God's ways can for a time be imitated by evil men, but eventually their deceits will be exposed.

4

The Wonder of God's Law

(Moses and the Ten Commandments)

Text: Exodus 20; Deuteronomy 5
Suggested Reading: Exodus 15:22—24:18;
32:1—40:38
Deuteronomy 4:1—12:32

"Moreover, the Lord showed great and distressing signs and wonders before our eyes against Egypt. . . . So the Lord commanded us to observe all these statutes . . ." (Deuteronomy 6:22, 24).

The lightning flashed, illuminating the mountain in a radiant electric glow. The thunder rumbled through the surrounding mountains and valleys, echoing as it sounded among rocky crags and rock-filled stream beds. Crashing, booming, shattering, blinding, deafening, rumbling, frightening signs drew the eyes of the newly emancipated Hebrews toward the dark cloud that lay over the mountain called Horeb or Sinai.

They had known that something special was about to happen, but nothing really could have prepared them for what they were now witnessing and hearing. For about two months they had been moving through the wilderness to the east of Egypt. It had not been an easy life. They had been hungry at times, but God had provided a white substance for them to eat. They called it manna. And they had been thirsty at times, and had been impatient with God for not responding to their needs as promptly as they expected.

But now they stood beneath the mountain where Moses, their great leader, once had seen a bush that burned without being consumed and where he had talked with God about His plan for deliverance of the Hebrews from Egypt. Now they also would hear the voice of the great God of Israel, Jehovah.

They had washed their clothes. They had refrained from sexual relations with their marriage partners. They had consecrated themselves, preparing in mind and spirit for the awesome thing that was soon to happen. And now the three days of preparation were past.

The Cloud

The lightning crackled from the cloud on the mountain above them, and the thunder clapped about them. They heard the sound of a loud, piercing trumpet call. It was the signal for them to approach the towering mountain.

Now fire was seen on the mountain, blazing up into the sky; and a great, billowing black smoke rose heavenward. Moses moved toward that trembling, groaning mountain as the people moved toward the barriers that had been erected to keep them from coming too close. They had vowed to Moses, "All that the Lord has spoken we will do!" (Exodus 19:8). Now His mighty voice spoke from the fire and the cloud and the mountain! Afterward they were to speak of what they heard from the voice of God as the "Ten Words." We have come to call them the Ten Commandments.

When God identified himself, saying, "I am the Lord your God, who brought you out of the land of Egypt," the minds of the people must have gone back to the wonders that Jehovah had performed in the midst of the people of Egypt, the plagues, and the miraculous parting of the Red Sea. They may have recalled how they had been set apart from the awful destruction of the plagues and how they had been spared from the destruction of the firstborn.

The Commandments

God's first commandment impressed on their minds that they were to be set apart from the polytheistic Egyptians and from the idolatrous people around them by their absolute devotion to one God. Jehovah was one. They were to love only Him, with all their heart, soul, and might (Deuteronomy 6:4, 5). He would brook no rivals (Deuteronomy 6:13-15). He was the only suitable object for worship. No gods were to be venerated but Jehovah and Him alone.

The second "word" concerned how they were to worship Jehovah. Strict prohibition was given against the making of images for worship and veneration, whether they be images of things in the sky like birds or celestial bodies, or things on the earth like animals or people, or things in the water like fish or mammals (Deuteronomy 4:15-19). Disobedience to this command would sow seeds of destruction within the race of Israel, but obedience to God's will would mean blessings innumerable (Exodus 20:5, 6).

The third "word" spoke of right relationship with God expressed by words and attitudes. The Hebrews were commanded never to use the name of God in an unworthy way, whether in false swearing, or in incantations and witchcraft, or in flippant talk.

The fourth "word" that the Hebrews heard thundering from Mount Sinai concerned a day of rest, the Sabbath, that was to be holy unto Jehovah. Jehovah himself, after His great work of creation, had established this precedent for His people.

These four commandments would, from that time forward, set the people of Israel peculiarly apart from their neighbors. When they were properly faithful, their loyalty to one God only, their abhorrence of idolatry, their respect for the name and person of God, and their sacred day of rest marked them as unique in history. These four were the commandments that spoke of their relationship with God. Then came six commandments that spoke of their relationship with their fellow men.

The first of these, the fifth "word," emphasized the importance of the family to God. The people of Israel were to respect, love, obey, and honor their parents. This commandment underlines the fact that one is not likely to be loyal to God or to one's own people if he does not first learn loyalty in the home. The family unit was to be a key factor in Israel's ability to take and hold the land of God's promise to them.

The sixth "word" spoke of the sacredness of life. "You shall not murder." One must not destroy the image of God in oneself or in another (Genesis 9:6). This did not rule out capital punishment (commanded in Exodus 21 and elsewhere in the law) or war (commanded in relation to the conquest of Canaan).

The seventh "word" that the people of Israel heard at Sinai demonstrated God's concern for the sanctity of the home. It prohibited infidelity on the part of husband or wife. Marriage was instituted by God. Vows taken before God were to be honored; bodies dedicated to Him were to be pure.

The eighth "word" spoke of God's concern for the sanctity of property. Stealing was an abomination to God, for it was a violation of the love and concern that one person ought to have for nother. Property cannot be divorced from people, for it represents part of the life of a person.

The ninth "word" spoke of God's concern for truth. The making of false accusation, lying, spreading false and damaging information, and the bearing of false witness were to be shunned by God's people.

The tenth "word" was somewhat different from the others, for it spoke not of an action but of an attitude. The people of God were not to make an idol of things by their desire to have what rightly belonged to another, whether it be a neighbor's property, servant, livestock, or any other possession.

All of these laws were not totally new to these wilderness wanderers. Certainly murder had been prohibited by the Egyptians and by other nations around them. But the Hebrews recognized that the law as delivered at Mount Sinai was uniquely God-given and sanctioned. Yet, ironically, within a matter of weeks many of them were dancing before a golden calf (Exodus 32).

The Calf

The calf was a pretty good likeness of the calves that had been worshiped in Egypt. Aaron himself had made it, probably covering a wooden structure with glistening gold from the rings and jewelry that were collected in the camp. Moses had been gone forty days, and the people wanted something tangible to lead them. So they made the calf and called it god and gave it credit for bringing them out of Egypt. And they made a feast, and they ate, and they drank, and they caroused before their idol.

God and Moses were together on the mountain. God knew what was going on below, and His anger was kindled. Moses pleaded with God not to destroy His wayward people from off the face of the earth (Exodus 32:9-14).

Moses came into the camp, furious for the honor of Jehovah. He carried in his hands two stone tablets that bore the "Ten Words," engraved by the very finger of God. And he cast them down before the people who had shattered the laws with their idolatry.

Moses burned the calf, ground it into powder, put this powder in water, and forced all the people to drink it. And the Levites were commanded to kill three thousand rebellious men who had committed this great sin.

The Covenant

Moses once again ascended the mountain of God, carrying with him two stone tablets that he had cut out himself. There, on the mountain again for forty days and nights, God renewed His covenant with Israel, "Behold, I am going to make a covenant. Before all your people I will perform miracles which have not been produced in all the earth, nor among any of the nations . . ." (Exodus 34:10). And Moses received detailed statutes and laws that he recorded in a book for his people (Exodus 34:27). Also he received on Mount Sinai the plan for the tabernacle, the portable tent that would be the center of religious ritual for the Hebrews until they were well settled in the promised land (Exodus 35:1—40:38).

The law was a wonder in the midst of Israel. Jesus said that its essence could be summed up in two parts. "The foremost is, 'Hear, O Israel; the Lord our God is one Lord; and you shall love the Lord your God with all your heart, and with all your soul, and with all your mind, and with all your strength.' The second is this, 'You shall love your neighbor as yourself.' There is no other commandment greater than these" (Mark 12:29-31).

The law was a great matter of pride to the Jews in later times, but they wrongly exalted having the law over obeying the law. The apostle Paul was to write much about the law and the gospel, comparing them and contrasting them. The law served to provide a standard for conduct and righteousness for the Jewish nation. It revealed man's sinfulness (Romans 3:19, 20); it revealed the awful nature of sin (Romans 7:8-13); it underlined the uniqueness of the only true God. But most of all it was designed to lead to Christ, in whom the believer could be justified by faith (Galatians 3:24). The law could not take away sin. It merely exposed it (Romans 7:7). It remained for the blood of the Lamb, the blood of Jesus, to provide cleansing from sin (Romans 8:3, 4).

Timeless Truths

- We no longer must wait at the bottom of the mountain to receive God's revelation. It has been put in our hands in the Scriptures. A little thunder and lightning might make us more appreciative, but, if we are anything like Israel, it probably would not make us more obedient.
- Moses beheld the glory of God, and it lit up his face. John tells us that Jesus was uniquely the expression of God's glory (John 1:14). How much does Jesus light up our lives?
- It took ten plagues to bring deliverance from Egyptian bondage, but it takes more than ten commandments to deliver us from unrighteousness. Only Christ can do that.
- Freedom is sometimes more difficult to handle than bondage.
- The people of Israel turned back to Egypt in their hearts. This was as abominable to God as if they had physically deserted Him and returned.
- It is in the nature of God to reveal His truth to man. At Sinai it was through "Ten Words." In Christ it is through the Word become flesh (John 1:14).
- The law was nailed to the cross (Colossians 2:14), but it is useful to our understanding of God's preparation for the coming of the Messiah.
- Jesus added an eleventh Commandment: "A new commandment I give to you, that you love one another, even as I have loved you, that you also love one another" (John 13:34).
- Often we are the most vulnerable to sin following moments of high religious experience.

5

The Wonder of God's Lovingkindness

(The Spies and the Wilderness)

Text: Numbers 13:25—14:45
Suggested Reading: Numbers 13—16;
Deuteronomy 1:20-46;
Psalms 103, 136; Hebrews 3, 4

"Pardon, I pray, the iniquity of this people according to the greatness of Thy lovingkindness" (Numbers 14:19).

There was real trouble in the camp, open division and impending riot. Some were picking up stones and calling for the death of two men who had just returned from a spying mission into Canaan. The place was Kadesh Barnea, an oasis just west of Edom, in the wilderness of Paran. The time was less than two years after the descendants of Jacob made their triumphal exit from the slave gangs of Egypt. It was a fateful day.

Return

Twelve good men, the best from each tribe, had been sent secretly into Canaan to scout it out before the impending move of the Hebrews into the land that God had promised would be theirs. Moses himself had told them to go to the south country and to the hills to note the military strength and numbers of the people, the nature of their fortifications, and the quality of their crops. And so they went. For forty days they had moved among the enemy. And now they had returned.

When word spread that they were back, the camp was alive with expectation. What had they found? What obstacles lay before the invaders? The people gathered to look at the large, luscious cluster of grapes and the pomegranates and the figs that the spies had brought back with them. To a people so long deprived of fresh fruit, these evidences of the fertility of the land were as precious as treasures of gold and silver.

Report

Good news! As God had promised them all along, this land was luxuriant and fertile, a land "flowing with milk and honey."

Bad news! The people occupying the land were strong, well fortified, numerous, and not likely to give up their land without a real scrap. "We are not able to go up against the people, for they are too strong for us," was the majority report (Numbers 13:31). "No way," ten of the spies nodded in agreement. "It's a land that devours its inhabitants and it will devour us. The people are huge, giants really. Beside them we felt like grasshoppers—and that's what we really are to them."

Rebellion

That was not what the nation had hoped to hear. Around the fires that night there was weeping and self-pity and grumbling against Moses for getting them into such a fix. There was great wringing of the hands and searching of the soul—and feelings of mutiny. "We might as well have died in Egypt," one said. "Or in the wilderness," said another. "Our wives and children will be taken from us and degraded by the enemy," opined still another. "We'll die on their swords." The murmuring grew, and the more they talked the more fearful they all became. No one paid the least attention to the two spies who urged them to go forward in the strength and power of Jehovah. Nobody seemed to remember that God had done some pretty startling things in Egypt with grasshoppers or locusts.

"We need a new leader," they said. "We need a new direction—back to Egypt. We've had it with Moses."

At the assembly that followed, Moses and Aaron fell prostrate on the ground, demonstrating their dismay at the lack of faith evidenced before them. Joshua, the spy from the tribe of Ephraim, and Caleb, the spy from Judah, urged the people to faithfulness. "If the Lord is pleased with us, then He will bring us into this land, and give it to us—a land which flows with milk and honey. Only do not rebel against the Lord; and do not fear the people of the land, for they shall be our prey. Their protection has been removed from them, and the Lord is with us; do not fear them" (Numbers 14:8, 9). The response of the assembly was immediate. They stooped over and picked up stones and prepared to silence these crazies.

Rejection

Suddenly there was a glow in the tent of meeting, that special tent where Moses met and talked with Jehovah. Jehovah's glory shone, and Jehovah's anger was kindled as He observed their lack of trust in Him! Moses pleaded for the people, and Jehovah demonstrated His lovingkindness once again toward this fainthearted nation (Numbers 14:11-21). But the faithless had lost their opportunity to see the land of promise. God would see to it that no one twenty years old or older, except Joshua and Caleb, would set foot in the land of Canaan. The others would die in the wilderness. For every day the spies had been in the land of Canaan, this hard-hearted people would be wandering a year in the barrenness of the waste places. Yet

God would not forget His promises. The day would come when their descendants would go into the land. God would teach them faith and trust through the difficulties of the desert and would purge His nation by the elimination of the faithless and fearful.

Reversal

Now the attitude of the Hebrews changed. What they had feared to do with the power of God with them they now dared to do with the power of God against them. The people mourned, confessed their sin, and mobilized for combat. Moses warned that this would be a suicide mission. They no longer had God with them. They would be crushed by their enemies, he said. And they were.

The writer of the New Testament book of Hebrews used this incident in the wilderness of Paran to urge the descendants of those wilderness Israelites to renewed faith (Hebrews 3:7—4:11). "Take care, brethren, lest there should be in any one of you an evil, unbelieving heart, in falling away from the living God" (Hebrews 3:12).

Reliance

Joshua and Caleb were in the minority, but they were right. They knew the task was not easy, but they also knew that with God on their side nothing was impossible. They remembered what God had done to the Egyptians and they had no doubt He could be counted upon to bring them victory over the Canaanites. They saw the obstacles and their comparative weakness as an opportunity for God to demonstrate His power. It is such people whom God can bless with victory.

The people, however, demonstrated the futility of life for those who are out of step with God. No matter what such people undertake, it will be a disaster.

God had been prepared to demonstrate His power against their enemies in the land of promise. Because of their disobedience and unbelief, however, He could demonstrate only His lovingkindness and forgiveness (Numbers 14:17-21). He would prepare them through the discipline of loss and through the chastening of the wilderness to trust Him as they had never trusted Him before. Moses wrote, "And you shall remember all the way which the Lord your God has led you in the wilderness these forty years, that He might humble you, testing you, to know what was in your heart, whether you would keep His commandments or not. And He humbled you and let you be hungry, and fed you with manna which you did not know, nor did your fathers know, that He might make you understand that man does not live by bread alone, but man lives by everything that proceeds out of the mouth of the Lord. Your clothing did not wear out on you, nor did your foot swell these forty years. Thus you are to know in your heart that the Lord your God was disciplining you just as a man disciplines his son" (Deuteronomy 8:2-5).

God's punishment of Israel came about because she did not know the ways of God (Psalm 95:10, 11). Yet God did not forsake His people and His promises to Abraham. He allowed His people to go through a period of great difficulty that was designed to teach them what they forgot at Kadesh Barnea, simple trust and obedience. It was a painful lesson for the nation, as all disciplining is likely to be. But it demonstrated clearly God's love for the people of His promises (Hebrews 12:6-11). The New Testament writer to the Hebrews urged Christians to hold to the truths of these events and apply them to their own lives. He wrote, "Let us therefore be diligent to enter that rest, lest anyone fall through following the same example of disobedience" (Hebrews 4:11).

These events at Kadesh Barnea represent a moment that required great faith and trust in the power and wisdom of God. It was a moment when it seemed that the forces of God were weak and powerless in the face of the overwhelming power of the enemy. Another such moment occurred outside the city of Jerusalem many years later. It was a moment that fulfilled God's ancient promise to Abraham, "And in you all the families of the earth shall be blessed" (Genesis 12:3). It was apparent defeat for the purposes of God, as God's only Son was nailed to a cross by Roman soldiers and crucified as a criminal.

But God's ways are unlike man's ways. God's lovingkindness turned the cross from a symbol of defeat to a symbol of victory. The blood of Christ was the blood of the perfect sacrifice for sin which made access to the riches of God's promises available to weak and sinful humanity. We sing with the psalmist, "For high as the heavens are above the earth, so great is His lovingkindness toward those who fear Him. As far as the east is from the west, so far has He removed our transgressions from us. Just as a father has compassion on his children, so the Lord has compassion on those who fear Him" (Psalm 103:11-13).

Timeless Truths

• Like the spies, we frequently know more about obstacles than we know about the power of God.

• To underestimate the power of God is worse than overestimating the power of the enemy.

• The report was a test for Israel. She flunked and went back to school for thirty-eight more years. The wilderness time was a teaching, toughening, and sifting time as the nation grew in dependence on God.

6

The Wonder of God's Victories

(Joshua and the Promised Land)

Text: Joshua 24
Suggested Reading: Joshua 1, 23, 24

"Then Joshua said to the people, 'Consecrate yourselves, for tomorrow the Lord will do wonders among you.' " (Joshua 3:5).

The old, wizened general called his battle-hardened people together for one last time. It seemed scarcely possible to him that he was now one hundred and ten years old. "Where," he thought, "has the time gone?"

He thought of his mentor, Moses, who had led the fathers and mothers of this band until he was one hundred twenty. Moses had died just before Joshua and the people had crossed the river Jordan to take the land of promise. *What would he think?* the old general wondered. Would he be satisfied with their battles, their victory, their new peace? Then the general's mind drifted back to Rephidim. They had just crossed the Red Sea on dry land and witnessed the destruction of Pharaoh's pursuing chariots when the waters crashed down on them. Suddenly, on that day so long ago, the Amalekites threatened them. Moses called Joshua to his side, saying, "Choose men for us, and go out, fight against Amalek" (Exodus 17:9).

So Joshua chose his best men and went out to fight. Above him on a hill stood Moses, his hands raised to

God. Joshua remembered that when that great man of God's arms fell, things went badly in the battle. He recalled how Aaron and Hur supported those mighty arms until Joshua prevailed. Joshua learned an important lesson that day—a lesson he continually spoke of in the hearing of his followers. It is not by might or cunning that victory is won, but by God's power.

Victory Recorded

Joshua remembered how faithfully Moses had recorded all that had befallen him and his people, and how Moses had read that record over and over to Joshua and to the nation of Israel. How Moses had loved that book! It contained the very law of God and the history of the wonders God had done in the midst of Israel. There was nothing in the whole world like that book.

Joshua's eyes became misty as he remembered. Every seven years, Moses had said, that precious record of God's words and wonders was to be read before the whole nation (Deuteronomy 31:10-13). Long before the land had been taken, Moses gave instructions for its reading and remembering at Mount Ebal (Deuteronomy 27).

Joshua thought of that day when he had accompanied Moses part of the way up Mount Sinai where Moses had received the law from the very hand of God. He remembered his forty-day spying expedition into Canaan, and how the fearful and unfaithful people had rejected his report when he came back. It was just before that spying expedition that Moses had changed the general's name from Oshea to Joshua, "Jehovah saves." How much had happened since then!

He remembered the sweet manna in the wilderness, God's special food provision for them. And the quails God had provided. And the sandals that did not wear out, despite the sharp, rocky path. He remembered what a special bond had developed between himself and Caleb during the thirty-eight years of seemingly aimless movement in the wilderness. They two watched as one by one the people died—the people who had been unfaithful and therefore had been forbidden entrance into the land of promise.

Joshua recalled Moses' final charge to him and his people as they encamped in sight of the land of promise at last. From the mountains above the Jordan they could see it stretched out beyond the river. Eager and excited, they wondered what lay ahead. Moses said, "It is the Lord your God who will cross ahead of you; He will destroy these nations before you, and you shall dispossess them. Joshua is the one who will cross ahead of you, just as the Lord has spoken. And the Lord will do to them just as He did to Sihon and Og, the kings of the Amorites, and to their land, when He destroyed them. And the Lord will deliver them up before you, and you shall do to them according to all the commandment which I have commanded you. Be strong and courageous, do not be afraid or tremble at them, for the Lord your God is the one who goes with you. He will not fail you or forsake you" (Deuteronomy 31:3-6).

How true that had been! God was like a swarm of hornets moving ahead of them into battle. The river Jordan parted for them just as the Red Sea had parted for their forefathers. Jericho's walls fell down flat before them. Ai was taken, coalitions of kings were defeated on every hand. There were still isolated pockets of resistance, but for all intents and purposes the land was now truly theirs. Through the rugged days of battle and conquest they had learned to be scrupulous in carrying out the commands of God, for it was a matter of life or death. When they disobeyed God their enemies prevailed, and when they obeyed they prospered beyond imagination. How often Joshua tried to instill in the thinking of his nation the words of God through Moses, "See, I am setting before you today a blessing and a curse: the blessing, if you listen to the commandments of the Lord your God, ... and the curse, if you do not listen to the commandments of the Lord your God (Deuteronomy 11:26-28).

Victories Recounted

Now it was Joshua's time to give his final charge to his comrades. He recounted the mighty wonders of God from the time of Abraham to the defeat of the Amorites. He spoke of how God had given them a wonderful land, ready prepared for them—fields they had not plowed, cities they had not built, cisterns they had not dug, vineyards they had not planted. Then, with all the vigor of his great heart, he challenged them: "Now, therefore, fear the Lord and serve Him in sincerity and truth; ... choose for yourselves today whom you will serve: ... but as for me and my house, we will serve the Lord" (Joshua 24:14, 15).

How his heart trembled as he heard the people's response to all his words: "We will serve the Lord our God and we will obey His voice"! (Joshua 24:24).

The people returned to their tents with the words of this mighty old warrior of God ringing in their ears. And, quietly, he died and was buried in the land of his inheritance. He would have been pleased by the words inscribed in the sacred book by the person whose task it was to bring an end to his chapter in it: "And Israel served the Lord all the days of Joshua and all the days of the elders who survived Joshua, and had known all the deeds of the Lord which He had done for Israel" (Joshua 24:31).

Victory Realized

It was Moses who gave the name *Joshua* to his younger protege. It was an appropriate name, for it was a reminder of the truth that Moses wanted impressed on the younger man's consciousness, "Jehovah is salvation." In later history, *Joshua* became a popular name. It was the name given by an angel for Mary's firstborn Son, the Messiah, for *Jesus* is the Greek equivalent of the Hebrew *Joshua* (Matthew 1:21).

There are many differences between the two men. Joshua was a man of war, Jesus was the Prince of Peace. Joshua was led by God, Jesus was God. Joshua was a conqueror of lands and cities, Jesus was conqueror of death itself.

There are similarities as well. The key to Joshua's strength was his unswerving loyalty to the will of God. This was characteristic of Jesus as well. Joshua led God's people into the promised land. That land over Jordan, in a metaphorical way, suggests Heaven. It is Jesus, uniquely, who leads the faithful into the land of eternal rest with the Father.

Joshua's name proclaimed the salvation of God. Jesus' name proclaimed it, His life demonstrated it, His death purchased it, and His resurrection sealed it.

Joshua won many great victories, but none was comparable to the victory of Jesus' resurrection (1 Corinthians 15:55-57). Jesus, by His resurrection, abolished death (2 Timothy 1:10). And because He rose from the dead we who believe also shall rise from the dead to be with God eternally (1 Corinthians 6:14, 2 Corinthians 4:14).

Timeless Truths

• When God goes before us, we need not fear what befalls us.

• God gives power and promise of victory, but we must do the fighting (1 Timothy 6:12).

• God keeps His promises.

• God has given man the power of choice. His choices have eternal consequences.

7

The Wonder of God's Patience

(Three Judges and the Enemies of Israel)

Text: Judges 3
Suggested Reading: Judges 1-3

"They, however, were rebellious in their counsel. . . . Nevertheless He looked upon their distress . . . and relented according to the greatness of His lovingkindness" (Psalm 106:43-45).

It was the best of times and the worst of times. Those who had fought beside Joshua in the first wave of conquest were now gone from the scene. It was an uncertain time covering perhaps three hundred to three hundred fifty years—a time of unfaithfulness when people turned away from God, and a time of faithfulness when individuals among the tribes of Israel rose to do God's bidding in carrying out His instructions to separate from the evil of the Canaanites.

Forgetfulness

There was a tragic generation gap, chronicled in the sacred book by these words: "And all that generation [Joshua and those who first took Canaan] also were gathered to their fathers; and there arose another generation after them who did not know the Lord, nor yet the work which He had done for Israel" (Judges 2:10).

The period of judges was like life on a seesaw. There would be that rising period of faithfulness and prosperity when the people obeyed God and trusted Him. Then would come that sinking phase of apostasy. "Then the sons of Israel did evil in the sight of the Lord" (Judges 2:11). There would follow a period of oppression by enemies within and without the land to which God had made them heir. Finally, a deliverer of faith would arise to call for a return to the Lord, and Israel would once again, with the power of the Lord in the midst, throw off the yoke of the oppressors. The chronicler put it this way: "And when the Lord raised up judges for them, the Lord was with the judge and delivered them from the hand of their enemies all the days of the judge; for the Lord was moved to pity by their groaning because of those who oppressed and afflicted them. But it came about when the judge died, that they would turn back and act more corruptly than their fathers, in following other gods to serve them and bow down to them; they did not abandon their practices or their stubborn ways" (Judges 2:18, 19). Because of their idolatry, God could not bless them as He wished to do.

Frustration

It was a time of testing for Israel (Judges 2:21, 22), a time of victory and a time of defeat, a time of faithfulness and a time of failure. Their enemies, the Philistines, the Sidonians, the Hivites, the Hittites, the Amorites, the Perizzites, and the Jebusites, to name a few, stubbornly remained in the land, a jabbing thorn in the side of the new nation. Attempts to live in peace with God's enemies led to intermarriage and compromise of Israel's loyalty to the one true God (Judges 3:6, 7).

God's anger with Israel for her rebellious ways led to His use of Cushan-rishathaim, the pagan king of Mesopotamia, who moved in from the east to afflict the people of Israel for eight years. Mesopotamia was the fertile land between the Tigris and Euphrates rivers. Little is known of this ruler with the enigmatic name meaning "man from Cush, he of the twofold crime" other than that he was successful against Israel because of its degenerate spiritual state.

There had been judges in Israel since its earliest day as a nation. Moses, on the advice of his father-in-law, Jethro, chose, not long after the exodus, able men to assist him in the management of the affairs of the nation. While the difficult disputes still came to Moses, the judges managed the more routine affairs (Exodus 18:24-26, Deuteronomy 1:9-17).

Faithfulness

Upon one such man, Othniel, the nephew of Caleb, that great warrior and man of faith, "the Spirit of the Lord came" (Judges 3:10). Othniel rose to leadership in the power of God. We are not told much about his preparations for revolt against the oppressions of the "man of Cush," but it seems clear that there must have been a spiritual reformation in Israel before there was a mobilization. Otherwise Othniel's success in battle would have been impossible.

Othniel, identified as the first of the prominent judges after the time of Joshua, made a difference. He drove out the oppressor, of course. And that was good. But more than that, he provided the spiritual leadership that made it possible for the Lord to bless Israel with forty years of "rest."

No sooner had Othniel died than the people of Israel slipped back into their corrupt ways. God's chastening was not long in coming. Eglon, a blubber of a man, with help from the Ammonites and Amalekites, took the area of Jericho. For eighteen years he held sway in that city where God had shown His power with such dramatic force to Joshua.

It was a sorry state of affairs. God had called upon His people to execute judgment on the evil people in these regions. But instead of being the sword of God, the Hebrews compromised with corrupt worship and evil.

Freedom

The revolt against the Moabites and their fat king, Eglon, began with an assassination. Ehud prepared carefully, concealing a short sword on his right thigh, beneath his cloak. Should Eglon's courtiers and bodyguards search him, they would not be likely to find his sword, since he had bound it in a place unusual for a right-handed person. For left-handed Ehud, however, it was perfect.

His mission was one ordinarily detested by his people, the presentation to the Moabites of the tribute required from the Hebrews. This time, however, Ehud undertook the task gladly. He had in mind giving the hated king something besides tribute.

If he was nervous as he passed through the bodyguard with his companions who carried the tribute, the Moabites did not notice. The Hebrews presented their tribute offerings as prescribed and returned by the way they had come. When the Hebrew party, however, reached Gilgal, Ehud turned back toward the Moabite palace, alone.

Perhaps it was the idols he saw at Gilgal that gave him the courage to follow through with the plan that he had been rehearsing ever since he began working on that special short sword he could feel lashed to his thigh. Those idols, those abominations in the face of Jehovah, could not be broken down as God had instructed His people until the domination of the Moabites was broken. Ehud was righteous for the name of Jehovah.

When he was ushered before Eglon, as he sat in the coolness of his roof chamber, Ehud said, "I have a secret message for you, O king" (Judges 3:19). Eglon told him to hold his peace until all were cleared from his chamber. It could not have been better for Ehud's plan.

"I have a message from God for you," Ehud repeated as he rose, drew his sword, and thrust it into the fat king's great, soft middle. While Eglon died, Ehud moved quickly. He locked the doors of the king's chamber, thereby gaining valuable time for his escape. Eglon's servants, supposing that the king had locked the door for privacy, did not want to disturb him.

Meanwhile, Ehud hurried to the hill country belonging to the tribe of Ephraim. There he blew the horn and assembled the Hebrews for battle. Swooping down from the hills, they seized the fords of the Jordan so that the Moabites in Israel could not escape. Ehud rallied his troops, shouting, "Pursue them, for the Lord has given your enemies the Moabites into your hands" (Judges 3:28). And indeed He had! When the battle was over, Israel had visited God's wrath on ten thousand of the Moabites.

Ehud's victory ushered in a period of eighty years of relative calm and normality for Israel. After Ehud died, however, the Philistines from the Mediterranean coast caused problems for Israel. This time Shamgar was the judge who rose up to deliver his people.

Fulfillment

God did wonderful things in the life of Israel. The Hebrews now were at home in their own land, and their possession of it was due to the fulfillment of God's promises in the wonders He had performed during the days of Moses and Joshua. But when those great leaders passed from the scene, there seemed to be no one of the same stature to remind God's people continually of the wonders of the past and the promises for the future. As the Hebrews settled into uneventful living, the real truths of life slipped into the back of their minds. They were influenced more by their neighbors than by their consciousness of God. As they slipped carelessly into sin, God allowed nearby tribes to defeat and oppress them. There is ever need for strong, uncompromising voices calling for strict conformity with the revealed will of God. When those voices are raised and heeded, God can pour out His blessings.

God did not forget His people and His covenant with them. He was always ready to receive them back and to bless them when they returned to Him, but sometimes their hardness of heart forced Him to give them hardness of life. The wonder of God's patience with His wayward children is clearly seen in the period of the judges.

Timeless Truths

• Many benefit when one person arises who is on fire for the will of God.

• When things go well it is easy to forget the Source of our prosperity. We begin to trust in ourselves and compromise with evil. Suddenly we find that God sends us adversity for our own good.

• It is impossible to do evil without evil consequences.

• The message of God is death to those who defy Him.

• Sometimes God allows evil to prosper in order to test the loyalty of the faithful.

• Foreign domination is not so bad as spiritual deterioration.

• God's blessings are sometimes delayed because of our inattention to Him.

• Hardness of heart leads to hardness of life.

8

The Wonder of God's Judgment

(Deborah and the Defeat of Sisera)

Text: Judges 4
Suggested Reading: Judges 4, 5

"For Thou hast girded me with strength for battle; Thou hast subdued under me those who rose up against me" (Psalm 18:39).

Her name meant "wasp," or perhaps "bee." She appears in the sacred record during one of those down periods of Israelite morality. She was a person of faith, imagination, and courage. She was a person, like Joan of Arc, to fire the imagination of her people and lead them to feats they scarcely thought possible. In the annals of Israel, Deborah has an honored and unique place.

Her story begins simply enough. She was accustomed to sit under a palm tree between Ramah and Bethel, in the hills of Ephraim. People came to her with their disputes, and she rendered judgment. It is doubtful if there were other women judges at the time, but there was something about her special character and wisdom that bred confidence in her. There must have been a special fire, the fire of holiness and dedication to God, that set her apart from those around her, whether men or women. The Bible says she was a prophetess, which means she was specially guided by the Spirit of God.

Israel, at least in her region, was no longer master of her own destiny. The Hebrews were vassals of Jabin, who ruled from his capital in Hazor. For twenty years he had been oppressing Deborah's people.

Jabin relied for the administration and subjection of his domain on his military commander, Sisera, who was stationed at a place called "Harosheth of the nations." Sisera's iron grip on the land was enforced by nine hundred iron chariots, the tanks of the day. The power of Jabin and Sisera seemed invincible to everyone—to everyone, that is, except the little "hornet" of Israel.

The Call

The Hebrews, who had done "evil in the sight of the Lord," cried out unto the Lord from the depths of bitterness they were experiencing at the hand of Jabin and his general, Sisera. People were afraid to be on the highways and to be in the fields. Disarmed, the people of Israel were helpless before their oppressors.

God heard the cry of His people and spoke to the situation through Deborah. She called Barak, a man whose name meant "lightning flash," and said, "Behold, the Lord, the God of Israel, has commanded, 'Go and march to Mount Tabor, and take with you ten thousand men from the sons of Naphtali and from the sons of Zebulun (Judges 4:6). Why God chose Barak we are not told. Was he skilled in war? Was he a natural leader? Was he a man of great faith? We are never told. His military knowledge, if he had any, would have told him that what she was suggesting was a suicide mission. But more compelling than common sense was Deborah's message from God, "And I will draw out to you Sisera, the commander of Jabin's army, with his chariots and his many troops to the river Kishon; and I will give him into your hand" (Judges 4:7).

The Challenge

As many a faithful person had done before him, Barak said yes to the call of the Lord through His messenger. But, for all his faithfulness, Barak insisted that Deborah accompany the Israelite force into battle. Perhaps he realized that her zeal for God would be as necessary to convincing ten thousand men to enlist in this venture as it had been to his own recruitment.

Deborah consented, but prophesied that the Lord would deliver Jabin's general into the hands of a woman. Barak probably interpreted this to mean that Deborah herself would be the instrument of Sisera's downfall, but things were to fall out in a different way.

So the "hornet" and the "thunderbolt" set out to raise an army. They were successful in enlisting volunteers from the tribes of Zebulun and Naphtali, with some from Benjamin, Ephraim, and Issachar (Judges 5:14, 15). It was a small army in comparison to what it might have been had all the tribes chosen to participate, but ten thousand it was that moved toward Mount Tabor to do battle with Sisera and his iron chariots.

The Conflict

Taking the high ground on Tabor, the Hebrews were in an advantageous position to encounter the army of Sisera, who hastily assembled his forces and came charging to the mountain with his rolling armament, those nine hundred chariots that he relied upon to instill fear into the hearts of his enemies. Though by comparison the Israelites were poorly armed, they went charging down the slope to battle. Perhaps they were protected somewhat by the wooded slopes of Mount Tabor from the iron chariots. It also seems possible that the heavy rains had so softened the terrain that the heavy-armed enemy found it extremely difficult to maneuver.

The Lord's forces routed Sisera, his chariots, and his army. Soon the stream of Kishon was clogged with the carnage of the battle. Barak, like a thunderbolt, pursued the fleeing Canaanites, slaying them with a great slaughter.

The Chase

So mired did Sisera's own chariot become that he jumped from it and ran from the battle on foot. That great machine of war in which he had taken so much pride was utterly useless in the terrain into which he had been drawn. So he resorted to the oldest of army tactics, putting one foot ahead of another.

He tired quickly. He panted into a Kenite camp and into the tent of a woman called Jael. Apparently the Kenites were somewhat neutral in the struggle between Jabin's people and the Hebrews. She welcomed Sisera into her tent and seemed to extend to him the traditional courtesies of hospitality. She gave him a rug to cover him and, because he was thirsty, some milk to drink. Having instructed Jael to lie if anyone should come seeking him, Sisera felt safe. Exhausted, he fell into a deep sleep from which he never awoke.

Jael took a tent stake and drove it with a hammer through his head. When Barak came rushing into the camp in hot pursuit of his enemy, Jael called him into the tent to see the dead Sisera. Thus Deborah's prophecy concerning the downfall of Sisera at the hand of a woman was fulfilled in dramatic fashion.

The Celebration

With this ignominious death of Sisera, his general, Jabin's power was before long extinguished. Deborah and Barak celebrated their victory with a song that ended, "Thus let all Thine enemies perish, O Lord; but let those who love Him be like the rising of the sun in its might" (Judges 5:31).

It is hard to see anything noble in the way Sisera met his death. Jael dealt treacherously with him and may well have violated the customs of hospitality of her day. On the other hand it may be that Sisera's entry into her tent while her husband apparently was away was itself a violation of mideastern custom. The Scriptures seem to indicate that she welcomed him. If he demanded or threatened, it is not recorded. Perhaps she, like the Israelites, had some scores to settle with the forces of Jabin and Sisera. Deborah, looking on her action as a bold stroke against the enemies of Israel, saw her deed as one of valor.

Deborah's song of victory not only exalted the deed of Jael, but it also gave praise to God for the little people, the peasants of Israel, whom God used. She called on the people to remember and recount the "righteous deeds of the Lord, the righteous deeds of His peasantry in Israel" (Judges 5:11).

Solomon closed his "words of the Preacher" thus: "The conclusion, when all has been heard, is: fear God and keep His commandments, because this applies to every person. Because God will bring every act to judgment, everything which is hidden, whether it is good or evil" (Ecclesiastes 12:13, 14).

In the experiences of Barak and Deborah we clearly see that God allows evil men and women to test His people, but there comes a time when He executes judgment on the oppressor. Deborah and Barak not only freed Israel from tyrannical and idolatrous rule, but they also executed God's judgment on evil. They recognized that their strength was from God and that their mission was God-ordained. Not to strike for God would have been to disobey their calling. There come times in the lives of Christians when they must step out on faith, trusting God for the outcome. Deborah and Barak stand as examples of those who allow God to work His marvelous work through them.

The psalmist must have been thinking of the likes of Jabin and Sisera and Deborah and Barak when he wrote, "Yet a little while and the wicked man will be no more; and you will look carefully for his place, and he will not be there. But the humble will inherit the land, and will delight themselves in abundant prosperity. . . . For the Lord loves justice, and does not forsake His godly ones; they are preserved forever; but the seed of the wicked will be cut off. . . . Wait for the Lord, and keep His way, and He will exalt you to inherit the land; when the wicked are cut off, you will see it" (Psalm 37:10, 11, 28, 34).

Timeless Truths

- Evil people are often done in by treachery.
- God's judgment on wickedness is sure.
- "For not by might shall a man prevail. Those who contend with the Lord will be shattered" (1 Samuel 2:9, 10).
- God's wonders are most graphically demonstrated against a background of weakness.
- Sometimes, like Sisera, we are in the greatest danger when we think we are safe (1 Corinthians 10:12).
- A spark of faithfulness can ignite a fire of freedom.
- The machines of men are powerless before the might of God.
- Women are powerful contenders in the battle with evil.

9

The Wonder of God's Strength

(Gideon and the Enemies From the East)

Text: Judges 7
Suggested Reading: Judges 6-8

"Then Gideon said to him, '. . . And where are all His miracles which our fathers told us about . . . ?' And the Lord looked at him and said, 'Go in this your strength and deliver Israel from the hand of Midian. Have I not sent you?' " (Judges 6:13, 14).

Gideon and Purah moved out into the night. They crept slowly, wary lest they send a boulder tumbling underfoot to betray their presence. Their mission took them into the very camp of the enemy, where one false step would mean death. They saw in the valley the campfires of the Midianites, the Amalekites, and the sons of the east. Silhouetted by the flickering firelight, camels almost without number grazed about the tents. Above them the stars shone, and around them the crickets called to one another. These two solitary men crept into the night, knowing not precisely for what they had come.

Gideon's Impossible Mission

God had sent Gideon on a mission to rid Israel of the marauding Midianites who had been wreaking havoc on them for seven years. Sweeping in from the east, the Midianites, along with the Amalekites and others from east of Jordan, had been like a plague of locusts, devouring everything in their path. They destroyed the crops, stole the livestock, laid waste the land. They were many in number, they and their great herds of camels, and it seemed that there was little the people of Israel could do to defend themselves but to hide in the caves and the mountains. It was a time of oppression that must have brought to the minds of many the bad old days that their ancestors had known in Egypt.

Gideon was working with the grain of his father, Joash, when that stranger first spoke to him. He was threshing covertly in the basin of a winepress so as not to alert the Midianites to his presence and the presence of new grain to be stolen. The regular threshing floors of the Hebrews were prime targets of the enemy. It was hardly a moment of great valor and courage on the part of Gideon. He was fearful and constantly looking over his shoulder for the enemy, keeping a low profile as he wielded his flail.

Gideon's Remarkable Commission

He was startled by that stranger whom he suddenly saw sitting under an oak near where he worked. But apparently the man was not an enemy, so Gideon was somewhat reassured.

The man said, "The Lord is with you, O valiant warrior" (Judges 6:12). Gideon must have looked around to see whom this stranger was talking to. He certainly showed no sign of valor at the moment, as he timidly hid his harvest from the eyes of the enemy. But the man seemed to be talking to him. And Gideon listened.

Sensing that this man was somehow an ally, Gideon poured out the frustration that he and so many of the Hebrews felt at their humiliation by the Midianites and the Amalekites. "Oh my lord, if the Lord is with us, why then has all this happened to us? And where are all His miracles which our fathers told us about, saying, 'Did not the Lord bring us up from Egypt?' But now the

Lord has abandoned us and given us into the hand of Midian'' (Judges 6:13).

The stranger cut through Gideon's self-pity and recrimination with a command that took his breath away: "Go in this your strength and deliver Israel from the hand of Midian. Have I not sent you?'' (Judges 6:14).

Gideon could scarcely believe the words he heard. He was from an insignificant family, and was its youngest member at that. Could it really be that he, Gideon, with all his weakness, was being called as was Moses at the burning bush? Was it possible that God himself was summoning Gideon to a task of deliverance?

Perhaps remembering the signs that Moses had experienced, the burning bush, the staff, the leprosy, and the water that turned to blood, Gideon asked for a sign to indicate unmistakably that the words being spoken were from God himself. When Gideon prepared a food offering and laid it on a rock near the oak, the man touched it with his staff. Suddenly fire leaped forth to consume the offering. Then the man was gone. Gideon, building an altar as he pondered the meaning of the words he had heard, knew unmistakably that he had joined the select few of history who had seen and spoken with the angel of Jehovah.

Gideon's Nocturnal Initiation

Things began to happen that Gideon had never expected. But before he could take on the enemy in the land, he had to take on the enemy in his own household. His father had erected an altar to Baal, the Canaanite god of the weather, and had erected by its side a totem dedicated to Asherah, the Canaanite fertility goddess. Now the Lord told Gideon to tear down the pagan altar and build another to Jehovah. On it he was to offer a sacrifice, using the wooden totem as wood for the fire.

The existence of this place of worship dedicated to evil idolatry was an indication of the sorry state of affairs in the religious life of Gideon's family and nation. Perhaps it represented an attempt by Joash to appease the Midianites and Amalekites more than it represented his own personal apostasy.

Gideon knew that what the Lord commanded was a dangerous deed. If he was caught desecrating the shrine of the gods of Canaan he would most certainly be put to death, even if the shrine belonged to his father. He did not know what his father's reaction might be. In a sense, Gideon's devotion to God was being tested by this command. Did he love God more than he did his father? More than life itself? Was his loyalty uncompromising? Was he as willing to take on the evil within Israel as the evil that was without?

The angel had called Gideon a "valiant warrior," but the first act of his mission demonstrated more fear than valor. Fearing to do God's bidding in the daylight, he chose to do it under cover of darkness. When the deed was discovered the next day and he was fingered as the guilty party, the vengeful men of the city came storming to Joash's house, determined to put Gideon to death. Joash, however, refused to cooperate with them, saying rather cannily, "If he [Baal] is a god, let him contend for himself, because someone has torn down his altar" (Judges 6:31). It was a significant remark that was to remain in the consciousness of Gideon and others through a name that ever after was applied to Gideon. That name was Jerubbaal, "Let Baal contend." This encounter demonstrated how incapable Baal was of doing that.

Gideon most certainly gained courage in this initiation into leadership and this adventure in trusting God, but he still had a great deal to learn about the ways of God. The stage was set for an even more dangerous confrontation with the enemy when the

Midianites, the Amalekites, and the sons of the east came over Jordan, 135 thousand strong, and camped, along with their great herds of camels, in the Valley of Jezreel (Juges 6:33; 8:10).

Gideon's Shared Vision

Gideon, moved by the Spirit of the Lord, blew the trumpet of war and sent messengers among the tribes. He could hardly believe it. Suddenly he found himself in command of thirty-two thousand fighting men.

Was it really true what was happening? Did God really want him to engage this powerful and numerous enemy? Did he really have the skills of leadership needed? Had God really called him?

Gideon's Miraculous Confirmation

He asked for another sign. He laid out a fleece on a threshing floor, that round, smooth area of rock where grain was winnowed, and asked God to give him a sign in the morning dew. If there was dew in the morning on the fleece and not on the ground around it, then, he said, he would know that it indeed was the Lord who was directing him. The following morning he found the fleece soaking wet and the ground dry. It should have been enough to convince him, but he was not satisfied. He reversed the stipulations. This time the fleece was dry and the ground around it was wet from the dew. There was no escaping the fact that God was going to use him, weak, fearful, hesitant, and uncertain though he was.

Gideon's fleece, like much that had gone before it, was a graphic illustration of his timidity and weakness. He had been threshing in the winepress because of fear of the enemy. He carried out God's command to break down the altar of Baal, but at night when no one could raise a hand to stop him. He just could not bring himself to trust the promised power of God for God's appointed task. God had given him clear signs and unmistakable instructions. But somehow the word of God was not quite enough for him. He wanted "something more," some further proof of God's commission and blessing. Gideon himself was aware that he was coming dangerously close to testing God. He introduced his request for the second sign with, "Do not let Thine anger burn against me that I may speak once more" (Judges 6:39). But God was patient with him and encouraged him in spite of his weakness. God had a plan for him that would use Gideon's weakness in a remarkable way to demonstrate God's wonderful strength.

As Gideon and Purah lay silently in the shadows of the enemy camp, Gideon must have thought of his own men in the hills above them. They had responded heroically to his call for mobilization against the Midianites, and it was a heady thing for him suddenly to find himself at the head of thirty-two thousand fighting men. But now only three hundred of them were left, and several times thirty-two thousand were sleeping in this wide-spreading camp of the invaders. Could he ever dare to lead his volunteers into battle against this huge force now camping in the valley by the hill of Moreh?

Gideon's Strange Proclamation

He could hardly believe he had done it. One day he had been recruiting, bending every effort to increase the size of his force. Then the next day he found himself sending people home, great bands of them. It was the Lord's doing, of course. He certainly would never have come up with an idea like that on his own. But the Lord told him to proclaim to his forces, "Whoever is afraid and trembling, let him return and depart from Mount Gilead" (Judges 7:3). He had worked so hard to assemble that force! He had been so pleased with the response from among the tribes! And then he saw two-thirds of his fighting men packing for home. God's ways were certainly strange.

As twenty-two thousand left, Gideon wondered if he ought to be marching at their head as they beat a retreat from the combat zone. If being afraid and trembling was a qualification for becoming a noncombatant, Gideon himself might well have qualified. These thousands, God explained to Gideon, were stripped from his army because they could not handle victory (Judges 7:2). Underestimating God's power at the outset, they were most likely to overestimate their own power at the finish.

Then God further reduced the size of Gideon's force. The ten thousand went to drink from a stream, and all were dismissed who knelt down or lay down and drank directly from the water. Gideon must have watched this test with increasing apprehension. Only an occasional soldier was so conscious of the possibility of enemy attack that he shunned the temptation to immerse his face and lips in the cool water. Only three hundred drank by cupping their palms and bringing the water to their lips. All the rest, nine thousand seven hundred of them, were sent home. The three hundred remaining were doubtless the most courageous men that were available. But would they dare to launch even a guerilla raid against an enemy that outnumbered them four hundred fifty to one?

Gideon thought of this as he and Purah lay in the darkness and strained to hear the talk beside the Midianite campfires on that fateful night. He was there because of fear. Who would not have been afraid? The Midianites, Amalekites, and sons of the east were as numerous as a plague of locusts, and their camels were as numerous as the sand on the seashore. Who would not have been afraid, except perhaps someone who knew in his heart the wonders that the Lord had performed in the past and who trusted God's word implicitly for the present?

God had given the enemy into his hands. Quite plainly He had told Gideon this. "But if you are afraid to go down," He had said, "go with Purah your servant down to the camp" (Judges 7:9-11). So in the darkness Gideon crept silently close to the enemy tents. There, in his fearful weakness, he received one more sign that the Lord was truly going to work a great wonder in their midst.

Gideon and Purah heard one of the Midianites relating a dream. The dreamer had seen a loaf of barley bread tumbling into the camp of Midian and knocking the tents flat. His companion interpreted the dream as meaning that Jehovah had given the camp of Midian into the hand of Gideon. These were the words that Gideon and Purah had come to hear. It was a sign from God that they would indeed be victorious.

Gideon's Victorious Confrontation

Gideon returned to his small band and weakened it still further, dividing it into three units of a hundred each. He gave careful instructions to the men. As he and Purah had done earlier, the three units crept close to the enemy. They hid their torches under pots so the sleeping men would not be alerted. In their hands, rather than instruments of war, there were instruments of music, trumpets. If any had doubts about the sanity of their leader, they nevertheless followed his directions.

Quietly they infiltrated the sleeping camp, moving stealthily past the careless outposts. Now!!! They blew their trumpets with all the breath they had in them. They smashed the clay pots that had concealed their torches. The trumpet blasts pierced the night! The bursting pots crashed in the darkness! The torches waved in awful, ominous proximity to the bewildered

Midianites. In a state of panic in the darkness, Midianite swords lashed out at anything that moved. The Hebrews shouted, "A sword for the Lord and for Gideon!" (Judges 7:20).

The Midianites ran this way and that, completely demoralized and out of control, killing one another in the night. They ran in panic, many heading toward the fords of the Jordan and their own territroy. But Gideon had alerted the Hebrews of the tribe of Ephraim. They took control of the fords, where they captured many and killed two great leaders of the Midianites, Oreb and Zeeb. Gideon pursued the fleeing Midianites and killed a number of their other leaders.

Gideon's experiences were a great example of how God can take weakness and turn it to strength. It is frequently in man's weakness that God can best demonstrate His power in human lives. Paul sensed this truth when he wrote, "Therefore I am well content with weaknesses, with insults, with distresses, with persecutions, with difficulties, for Christ's sake; for when I am weak, then I am strong" (2 Corinthians 12:10).

Gideon began his journey to fame too fearful to go near a threshing floor lest the enemy harm him. God moved him out to a threshing floor. There, too fearful to go near the enemy camp, Gideon was granted signs of God's leading. When he was near the enemy camp, too fearful to engage them in battle, God strengthened him still more. Finally he arrived where God wanted him to be, in the camp of the enemy, filled with trust in God. Despite his weakness, God patiently led Gideon one step at a time toward the goal He had for him.

So impressive was Gideon's victory that the people desired to make Gideon a king. His emphatic rejection, "I will not rule over you, nor shall my son rule over you; the Lord shall rule over you" (Judges 8:23), showed clearly that he had been prepared by God to handle the victory when it came. It is too bad that he apparently was not able to pass the lessons of his life along to his son, Abimelech (Judges 9).

It is interesting to note that Gideon's first step of obedience to God's will was a night attack on the pagan gods of his father. His call was confirmed by the night dew. His heart was strengthened by a night foray into the enemy camp, and his victory was won in a night attack. Yet the appropriate symbol for Gideon is a torch. God used a small light in immense darkness to demonstrate His strength and power. He still does! (Matthew 5:14-16).

Timeless Truths

• God often makes unlikely choices to bring about His purposes.

• " 'Not by might nor by power, but by My Spirit,' says the Lord of hosts" (Zechariah 4:6).

• It is not the size of the force but the power of the Spirit in the force that makes the difference.

• God hears the cries of His people (Judges 6:6-10).

• Disobedience enslaves (Judges 6:10).

• All true strength is from Jehovah (Judges 6:14).

• If we do not believe that God can help us, and He does, we are prone to take the credit for ourselves (Judges 7:2).

• Those who are not spiritual cannot be trusted with great victories.

• Trusting faith is better than trusting fleeces.

• "But God has chosen the foolish things of the world to shame the wise, and God has chosen the weak things of the world to shame the things which are strong, and the base things of the world and the despised, God has chosen, the things that are not, that He might nullify the things that are, that no man should boast before God" (1 Corinthians 1:27-29).

10

The Wonder of God's Gifts

(Samson and the Philistines)

Lesson Text: Judges 16
Suggested Reading: Judges 13-16

"Seek the Lord and His strength;
Seek His face continually.
Remember His wonders which He has done"
(Psalm 105:4, 5).
"He performed wonders while Manoah and his wife looked on"
(Judges 13:19).

In the dungeon of Gaza, he sweated against the huge millstone to which the bronze chains held him. Round and round like a blindfolded ox on a threshing floor, he plodded through the long days and nights of his agony. His expression was as blank as his eyes, those empty sockets where his eyeballs once had been.

As he pushed methodically against the heavy beam extending from the millstone, he heard the jeers of his masters and an occasional crack of a whip. He had become a tourist attraction to the Philistines, who made it a point to stop by to ridicule this once fearsome hulk of a man.

During the long, tedious hours, Samson had plenty of time to review his life. No one could say it had not been exciting and extremely unusual, even if it was ending tragically. Samson's mind drifted away from the sounds of his oppressors, the Philistines who had been tormenting Israel for forty years, to the peace and promise of his childhood home.

The Blessed Baby

Samson remembered his father, Manoah, and the care he had had for Samson as a child. He remembered his mother also, that godly woman who had so tried to impress on him his specialness. She delighted in telling him of the two visits of the angel of the Lord who had announced Samson's imminent birth, despite the fact that she had been barren. His mother told him how slow Manoah had been to recognize that the visitor was the angel of the Lord, and how concerned he had been when he had seen his angel ascending in the flame from an altar where he had laid out an offering. Most of all, however, his parents impressed on him the fact that he was set apart as a Nazarite, special to Jehovah. His hair was not to be cut. How often his parents had called attention to the fact that he was a man of destiny, a child of prayer!

Yet there had been a rebellious streak in him, a certain childlike abandon. His youth was filled with not-too-smart escapades and derring-do. Life was a bit of a lark for a youth whose strength set him apart from the run-of-the-mill.

Now, as he ran the mill, he remembered how upset his parents had been when he took a wife from among the hated Philistines. His parents were right, of course. It was a bad thing to do. But he knew, somehow, that God was going to work His purposes even through this (Judges 14:4).

The Victorious Victim

The whole wedding had been a fiasco. His parents went to Timnah reluctantly. Samson, however, was enjoying himself immensely, as usual. Earlier, on a trip to Timnah, he had been surprised by a lion along the path. The poor lion ended up lying alongside the path, torn by the powerful arms of Samson. Afterward a swarm of bees entered the dead carcass. On a later trip, Samson went aside to relive his exploit and found the honey-filled lion. He scooped the honey out and went on along to his parents, his sticky hands dripping all the way. Apparently he knew how to rob the bees without getting stung.

The wedding feast was a blast for the young, muscular groom. The Philistines sent thirty young men to celebrate the feast with him. In the course of the evening, Samson made a wager with them that they could not guess a riddle: "Out of the eater came something to eat, and out of the strong came something sweet" (Judges 14:14).

When the Philistine guests failed to come close to a solution after three days of earnest cogitation, they began to fear that they might have to pay off their wager by giving him the thirty linen wraps and the thirty changes of clothing they had wagered.

The Philistine youths applied pressure to Samson's young wife. She opened the floodgates of her eyes day by day, wailing, "You don't love me!" At last he could stand it no longer. It was the seventh day, the last day of the allotted time, when he shared his secret with her.

When his antagonists, on the seventh day, happily chimed, "What is sweeter than honey? And what is stronger than a lion?" he knew that his wife had betrayed him. In a rage he went out, slew thirty of the Philistines of Ashkelon, and delivered their raiment to the men of Timnah.

Samson never seemed to be very fortunate in his dealings with women. He remembered how he had destroyed the fields of the Philistines by tying torches onto the tails of foxes and sending them running through the crops. He had laughed at that. It had been in vengeance for an injustice visited upon him by his Philistine father-in-law at Timnah. He had given Samson's wife to another man. Following Samson's fiery evening, the Philistines, aware that Samson had truly been wronged, showed that they too could play with fire. They burned his wife and her father.

Samson's life seemed motivated primarily by revenge, but he nevertheless seemed to be prompted by the Spirit of the Lord in his harassment of the pagan and sinful Philistines. He remembered how God had provided water for him at Lehi, following the time he killed a thousand of the Philistines with the jawbone of a donkey. Now in the dungeon of Gaza, Samson looked back on those days of strength and power as if from a great distance.

Gaza too had been a place where he had astounded the Philistines. They felt sure they could take him after he spent a night there with a harlot. Thinking they had shut him in the city, they did not reckon that he might tear down the city gate itself. But he did, both it and its posts on either side. And he deposited the great gate and its posts, a little reminder of his visit, on a hill that faced toward Hebron. He wondered how many men it had taken to return it to the city.

The Disastrous Disclosure

Yes, he had never been wise in his dealings with women. Delilah had led him to his worst blunder. Oh, he had dallied with her and delighted in tricking her when she tried to discover the secret of his great strength. But eventually he had made the mistake of opening his heart to her. "A razor has never come on my head, for I have been a Nazarite to God from my mother's womb. If I am shaved, then my strength will leave me and I shall become weak and be like any other man" (Judges 16:17).

It was a fatal disclosure. While he slept, she had his hair cut and delivered him to his enemies. He soon was aware that things were not as before. The Lord had departed from him.

All these things went through his mind as he applied his strength against the dead weight of the millstone. He had noticed of late, however, that his strength seemed to be returning. His hair was growing once again. The Philistines seemed not to notice or care.

Suddenly he was unchained from the millstone and forced to stumble up the steps from the dungeon. He felt the sun on his face. His name meant "sunny," but the sun had not reached him in a long time.

The Last Laugh

They led him into the court of the temple of Dagon where the Philistines had assembled for a great festival to their god. They praised Dagon for delivering their arch enemy into their hands. They laughed at him as they made him stumble blindly about to amuse them. They mocked his weakness and delighted in his humiliation before them.

Samson found himself the butt of their amusement, but he realized that it was really Jehovah that they were mocking. Though Samson had indeed been a judge in the name of Jehovah, his life had not fulfilled the high promise his parents had dreamed of. Three thousand Philistines on the roof of the temple taunted him, and other thousands were below. Samson found himself at the architectural center of the building. Feigning the need to rest, he had a boy place his hands on the two pillars that supported the weight of the building. He felt the strength of Jehovah rising within him as of old as he prayed,"O Lord God, please remember me and please strengthen me just this time, O God, that I may at once be avenged of the Philistines for my two eyes" (Judges 16:28).

He began to exert his strength against those two pillars, one bulging arm against one pillar and the other arm against the other pillar. "Let me die with the Philistines!" he prayed in a shout. There was a groan-

73

ing as the column began to budge. Then there was a shout of fear from above as the great house of Dagon began to topple, its weight impacting on those who were within and below. With a great, sickening rumble the huge temple collapsed in a heap of stone and death. A great company of Dagon worshipers perished. In this strange and tragic way, Samson's twenty years of judgeship came to an end. As the angel had foretold before he was born, he began to deliver Israel from the Philistines (Judges 13:5), but he did not finish the job.

If ever there was a man set apart from the ordinary it was Samson. From his birth to his death, he was indeed different. If Gideon was a weak man made powerful by the blessings of God, then Samson was a strong man made weak by the foolhardiness of man. His great gifts seem to have been dissipated. His strength was more physical than spiritual. Only in death did he seem to take God's purpose for his life seriously. And even then he was thinking more about vengeance than the vindication of the name of Jehovah.

Yet it must be said that Samson set something in motion besides the two columns of the Dagon temple. He was instrumental in beginning the deliverance of Israel from the abomination of the Philistines, a task that was to continue on into the days of Saul and David. Though his personal motives do not seem to have been of the highest sort, we must remember that God was using this strong man for His own purposes (Judges 14:4). Samson was listed by the Hebrew writer in the New Testament as one of the heroes of the faith "who by faith conquered kingdoms, performed acts of righteousness, obtained promises, shut the mouths of lions, quenched the power of fire, escaped the edge of the sword, from weakness were made strong, became mighty in war, put foreign armies to flight" (Hebrews

11:33, 34). Yet Samson must also stand as a model of wasted potential, one of the gifted of whom much is required, a profligate whose tragedy is the more dramatic because of the resources he squandered.

God somehow brought sweetness from this strong, often petty man. There is a special beauty in the rebirth of his strength that seems to speak of God's continuing love and restoration in the aftermath of disobedience. Samson was less that he could have been, but by the grace of God he was more than he might have been.

Timeless Truths

• Those who open their hearts to evil people can expect to be shorn.

• Those who masquerade as our friends can do more harm to us than our avowed enemies.

• There is special tragedy in squandered natural gifts.

• Those who play with fire get burned.

• Special abilities may set us apart from others. They do not, however, guarantee wisdom.

• There is no more tragic realization than that the Spirit of the Lord has departed.

• Strength is no substitute for nobility.

• If you live in the enemy camp, do not be surprised if the enemy blinds you.

11

The Wonder of God's Redemption

(Ruth and Her Adopted People)

Lesson Text: Ruth 3
Suggested Reading: Ruth 1-4

"O Thou my God, save Thy servant who trusts in Thee" (Psalm 86:2).
"In the day of my trouble I shall call upon Thee, for Thou wilt answer me" (Psalm 86:7).

The closing chapters of the book of Judges present a veritable rogue's gallery of idolaters (Micah), idolatrous priests (the Levite of Micah), thieves (the men of Dan), harlots (the Levite's concubine), sodomites, rapists, and murderers (the men of Gibeah), and vengeful butchers (the Levite husband of the concubine). The book closes with an account of a bloody civil war that pitted brother against brother and nearly destroyed the tribe of Benjamin. Finally, the swirl of intrigue, vengeance, waste, deceit, idolatry, unfaithfulness, jealousy, murder, and bloodshed comes to an end, and we are granted a gentle interlude before the Biblical record moves toward the establishment of kingship in Israel.

The book of Ruth is an account of loyalty and love, tenderness and consideration, encouragement and kindness, faith and trust. It is an island of good in a turbulant sea of intrigue. It seems the more beautiful because of its doleful surroundings. The scene for the book is that most unsettled of times, the period of the

76

judges. The events recounted are not the great events of clashing arms and falling kingdoms that are the usual subject matter of the book of Judges. Rather, Ruth beautifully records the story of indivdiual people. What they did may seem pedestrian, but through simple loyalty, trust, and kindness they planted seeds of character that flowered in the line of David and of the Lord Jesus himself.

Refuge

Things had been bad in Bethlehem. A famine ravaged the land. Elimelech, his wife, Naomi, and their two sons, Mahlon and Chilion, reluctantly left the hungry land of their inheritance and headed east across the Jordan and south into the land of Moab. As they journeyed they remembered how Moses and their forefathers had passed through this land to the east of the Dead Sea on their journey to the land of promise, a land no longer was flowing with milk and honey, at least in Bethlehem of Judah.

Elimelech and Naomi must have wondered what might happen in their lives and the lives of their two sons in this foreign land. The Moabites were distant relatives of the Hebrews through their descent from Lot, Abraham's nephew (Genesis 19:30-37). Their language was virtually the same as the one Elimelech and his family spoke, so the adjustment might not be too hard.

They seemed to fit right in, but tragedy struck with the death of Elimelech. Naomi was left to make the arrangements for the marriage of her two sons. She felt good about her choices, and she was pleased with her relationship with her two daughters-in-law, Orpah and Ruth. When death unexpectedly took her two sons, however, Naomi was deeply grieved and extremely lonely. Her daughters-in-law were lovingly helpful to her during the time of their grief.

Return

When she heard that there was now food in her girlhood home of Bethlehem, Naomi made up her mind to return to her relatives. Moab had been a place of survival for her, but it also had been a place of deep grief. Now, she felt, she must put all that behind her and begin life once again. No place would be so good for that as the home of her childhood. The only thing that bothered her about her decision was saying good-bye to her two daughters-in-law. There had developed a special bond among them as they had shared in the joy of marriage and the sorrow of death. They had stood with her and shared in her sorrow for her beloved sons.

The three of them walked together toward the borders of Moab, deep in their own introspection. Finally the time came for parting. Naomi said to them, "Go, return each of you to her mother's house. May the Lord deal kindly with you as you have dealt with the dead and with me" (Ruth 1:8). She kissed them and they three embraced and wept together.

The two Moabite daughters-in-law loved Naomi deeply. Her life and love had been such that they loved her as much or more than their natural mothers. They expressed their desire to accompany her into the uncertainties of her future, even as they had accompanied one another in the sorrow of the immediate past. She urged them to return to their people. They were young enough still to find husbands and bear children. She loved them and wanted the best for them, as if they were her own daughters. No selfishness clouded her motives. She did not think of herself but of them. That had been a special characteristic they had noted in her from the very beginning. That was one reason they loved her so much. She accepted her fate as the judgment of the Lord and was willing to go on with Him into the loneliness of solitary old age.

Orpah reluctantly kissed her and prepared to return to her family. Ruth, however, refused to desert Naomi. Her words of loyalty, simply stated, have become classic words of fidelity: "Do not urge me to leave you or turn back from following you; for where you go, I will go, and where you lodge, I will lodge. Your people shall be my people, and your God, my God. Where you die, I will die, and there I will be buried. Thus may the Lord do to me, and worse, if anything but death parts you and me" (Ruth 1:16, 17).

Joy and sorrow mingled in the homecoming when Naomi and Ruth at length arrived at Bethlehem. The meaning of Naomi's name was "pleasant" and such her nature had always been. But she saw in what had befallen her the affliction of the Almighty and said she ought to be called Mara, "bitter," instead.

Relief

Despite the fact that many had happily received them, life was not immediately easy for Naomi and Ruth. Ruth resolutely undertook to provide for herself and her mother-in-law. She arose early and went to the fields to gather grain behind the harvesters. The law of Moses commanded the reapers to leave the gleanings and the corners of the fields for the needy and the strangers (Leviticus 19:9, 10). It was a good system of welfare, for it required work from those in need.

Ruth, by chance, found her way to the field of a certain Boaz, a wealthy relative of her father-in-law. He notcied her diligence in the field and knew of her fidelity to Naomi. Boaz was considerate of her, urging her to come again to his fields, assuring her safety among his reapers, and seeing to her personal comfort. He said, "May the Lord reward your work, and your wages be full from the Lord, the God of Israel, under whose wings you have come to seek refuge" (Ruth 2:12). He called her to eat with him and the reapers; and when he was giving instructions to his workers, he told them to make sure that plenty of grain was left for Ruth.

She worked throughout the day and beat out the barley in the evening. She could hardly believe it—a whole ephah of barley for her day's work! Naomi could hardly believe it either. But when Ruth recounted the special treatment she had received from Boaz, Naomi began to see the hand of the Lord in all that was happening. Boaz was a near relative.

Naomi thanked God for Boaz, saying, "May he be blessed of the Lord who has not withdrawn his kindness to the living and to the dead" (Ruth 2:20). And perhaps she smiled a little as her mind raced ahead. Perhaps Ruth, this sweet, hard-working, loyal companion of hers, whose very name meant "companion," would one day soon have a man companion of her own. Ruth continued among the reapers through the barley and wheat harvests, while Naomi smiled and thought of what she could do to bring about a match.

Redemption

Naomi determined to give things a shove during the winnowing season. She knew that Boaz would be sleeping at the threshing floor, as was the custom, to guard the grain. She saw to it that Ruth was bathed, perfumed, and decked out in her most attractive attire. She instructed Ruth to wait until Boaz lay asleep before she crept near to lie down at his feet. There was a hint of eagerness and simple trust in the wisdom of her mother-in-law as Ruth said, "All that you say I will do" (Ruth 3:5).

The harvest was always a special time of rejoicing and merriment. Boaz enjoyed the festivities of the winnowing time. Then, tired, he dropped into a peaceful sleep. He was startled, however, when he woke in the night to find a woman lying at his feet. To his anxious question, "Who are you?" she replied that she was Ruth, a close relative. "So spread your covering over your maid," she added. It was a modest way of asking him to fulfill the law that required a man to take the widow of a near relative as his wife, and through her to raise up children to his dead kinsman (Deuteronomy 25:5-10).

Boaz was complimented that she had come to him. He respected her judgment. How could he do otherwise? She had chosen him. He had seen and heard of her excellence. He was pleased with the idea of making her his wife, but he was an upright and righteous man who would not let his desires supersede the commands of God. There was a closer kinsman who would have to be consulted.

The following day he spoke with the closest male relative of Ruth's dead husband. That man had the first right to take Ruth as his wife and to buy the property that Naomi was offering for sale. If he would do this, the first son born to him and Ruth would not be considered his son, but the son of Ruth's first husband, and he would inherit the property. At first the kinsman seemed inclined to exercise his right, but soon he changed his mind. He did not want to mortgage his own property in order to get another field that he would have to pass on to a son who legally would be the son of another man.

Boaz was next in line. Gladly he claimed the right to redeem the property of Elimelech, to take Ruth as his wife, and to agree that her son would be the heir of her first husband, Mahlon.

Reward

With the good wishes of the city fathers and the people of Bethlehem, Boaz took Ruth for his wife. What joy was Ruth's and Naomi's when she bore a son! Neighbor women joined in the rejoicing, and they called him Obed. The name means either a worshiper or a servant. Perhaps it means a servant here, for the women said he would take care of Naomi in her old age (Ruth 4:15). The women of Bethlehem said also, "Blessed is the Lord who has not left you without a redeemer today, and may his name become famous in Israel" (Ruth 4:14). And indeed his name did become famous. Ruth's baby became the father of Jesse, who became the father of David, the great king of Israel. And in this blessed line came Joseph, who cared for young Jesus (Matthew 1:1-16; Luke 3:23-38).

The story of Ruth demonstrates graphically that God rewards loyalty and faithfulness. Ruth's warm, trusting, loving spirit created an atmosphere in which God was pleased to bless her and to bless the nation of Israel through her. Though she was a foreigner, God worked through her His wonders. Her line became the most important blood line of Israel. Her loyalty brought honor, happiness, and contentment. Righteous dealing, hard work, loyalty, and respect brought their rewards in Ruth's life, in that of Naomi, in that of Boaz, and in that of their descendants.

It is interesting that Boaz played the part of a "redeemer." He bought back the land that had formerly belonged to Elimelech, but would have gone to another family if there had been no heir in Elimelech's family. By taking Ruth for his wife, he became in a sense a redeemer of the life of his kinsman Elimelech, or at least of the family of Elimelech. For the family line would have ended if Boaz had not continued it by fathering a son who would legally be the son of Mahlon and grandson of Elimelech.

The ancient Hebrew custom of redemption turns the mind of the Christian to the special work of Jesus, the Redeemer. It was Jesus who paid the price of our redemption. Therefore God "delivered us from the domain of darkness, and transferred us to the kingdom of His beloved Son, in whom we have redemption, the forgiveness of sins (Colossians 1:13, 14). It was Jesus, our near kinsman, who took us who were destined for death and brought us to life again so that we might inherit the promises of God.

Timeless Truths

- Loyalty is a priceless gift.
- Boaz did that which the law and custom demanded, even if it meant delaying his own desires. There is patience and orderliness in the conduct of the good.
- People know us through our actions. Good deeds are praise to God and an honor to our name (Ruth 3:11).
- Goodness carries its benefits from generation to generation.
- Love, faithfulness, loyalty, and concern break down national barriers and overcome prejudices.
- There is special sweetness in the joys that follow adversity.

12

The Wonder of God's Faithfulness

(Samuel and Transition to Kingship)

Lesson Text: 1 Samuel 12
Suggested Reading: 1 Samuel 1-12

"Thou wast a forgiving God to them, and yet an avenger of their evil deeds" (Psalm 99:8).

The high priest thought she was drunk. The disconsolate woman prayed so earnestly from the troubled recesses of her heart that Eli, the high priest who sat near the entrance of God's tabernacle at Shiloh, mistook her agonizing tears and the silent movements of her lips for drunken madness. At his reprimand she replied, "I have drunk neither wine nor strong drink, but I have poured out my soul before the Lord" (1 Samuel 1:15).

Indeed she had. Not only had she poured out her humiliation at not having a child, but she had made a vow to God: "O Lord of hosts, if Thou wilt indeed look on the affliction of Thy maidservant and remember me, and not forget Thy maidservant, but wilt give Thy maidservant a son, then I will give him to the Lord all the days of his life" (1 Samuel 1:11).

Answered Prayer

God heard and answered Hannah's prayer. She had a son. She called him Samuel, a name that acknowledged the fact that God hears the prayers of His people. How her heart was lifted up! She prayed a great prayer of thanksgiving for the wonderful love of God shown in His response to her prayer (1 Samuel 2:1-10). "My heart exults in the Lord; my horn is exalted in the Lord!" she cried in her happiness.

Was any remorse for her vow in Hannah's mind as she prepared to fulfill it by giving her firstborn son over to the high priest and those who cared for the tabernacle? If there was, we are not told of it. She held the baby to her breast and cuddled him and cooed to him until he was weaned. Then, without looking back, she set out on her journey to Shiloh. There she presented the young boy to Eli with these words: "For this boy I prayed, and the Lord has given me my petition which I asked of Him. So I have also dedicated him to the Lord; as long as he lives he is dedicated to the Lord" (1 Samuel 1:27, 28).

Righteous Youth

And it was true. As long as Samuel lived he was uniquely dedicated to the work and purposes of God. Visited occasionally at times of sacrifice by his father and mother, who brought him clothes and presents (1 Samuel 2:19), Samuel worshiped the Lord at Shiloh and grew up among the priests who served in the ceremonies of the tabernacle.

Samuel seems to have escaped the corruption of Eli's worthless sons (1 Samuel 2:12-25). The short record of his growth to maturity sounds similar to what Luke (2:52) wrote in his account of the boyhood of Jesus: "Now the boy Samuel was growing in stature and in favor both with the Lord and with men (1 Samuel 2:26).

Samuel's virtue contrasted so dramatically with the iniquity of Eli's two sons, Hophni and Phinehas, that it became increasingly clear that God had raised up

Samuel to carry on the work of God in their stead. This was confirmed by the very voice of God (1 Samuel 3:1-18). The chronicler noted, "Thus Samuel grew and the Lord was with him and let none of his words fail. And all Israel from Dan even to Beersheba knew that Samuel was confirmed as a prophet of the Lord. And the Lord appeared again at Shiloh, because the Lord revealed Himself to Samuel at Shiloh by the word of the Lord" (1 Samuel 3:19-21).

Man in the Middle

Samuel came at a time of transition. He was the last of the judges (1 Samuel 7:15) and the first of the prominent prophets after the days of Moses (1 Samuel 3:20). He bridged the gap from the chaotic times of the judges to the establishment of the kingdom under Saul. He was perhaps the greatest man of God since Moses. Unlike many of the other judges, he seems to have had no blot on his personal character, unless it be that he, like Eli before him, produced some irresponsible sons (1 Samuel 8:3).

The major enemy of Israel at that time was the Philistines. They even succeeded in capturing the ark of God, to their own discomfort and sorrow (1 Samuel 4—6). Like Moses before him, Samuel called upon the Hebrews to repent from their idolatry that they might be delivered from the oppression of their enemies (1 Samuel 7:3). He and the people saw miraculous deliverance when they relied on the power of God (1 Samuel 7:9, 10).

Reluctant King-maker

It is as a king-maker, however, that Samuel is primarily remembered. It was he who anointed both Saul and David to the kingship. His life intertwined with those of these two remarakble men during the formative days of the kingdom.

Samuel was not at all pleased when the leaders of Israel came to him at Ramah with their request that he appoint a king over them. He saw their desire as a rejection of his leadership, but God said, "Listen to the voice of the people in regard to all that they say to you, for they have not rejected you, but they have rejected Me from being king over them" (1 Samuel 8:7).

To the leaders, a king seemed to be the obvious answer to the problems they had experienced during the period of the judges. A king, they thought, would unite them, and give them increased power against their enemies. Though Samuel clearly pointed out the human costs of a kingdom (1 Samuel 8:10-18), the leaders were sure they knew what they wanted. "No," they said to Samuel's plea that they continue to rely wholly on God for their deliverance, "but there shall be a king over us, that we also may be like all the nations, that our king may judge us and go out before us and fight our battles" (1 Samuel 8:19, 20).

There were obvious problems in Israel, especially in relation to the Philistines. But Israel forgot the lessons of her wonderful history. Again and again God's messengers had sought to impress the simple truth that if they served, obeyed, and sought God they would prosper, and if they rebelled, disobeyed, and forgot God they would be oppressed. They thought a king might enable them to prosper in spite of themselves, but Samuel knew better. What a tragedy! They wanted to forfeit their most wonderful possession, the possession that made them unique among all nations, the personal leadership of God, in order to be led by a king like everyone else.

Preacher of Righteousness

Chapter 12 of 1 Samuel contains Samuel's great call for dependence on the truths of God. He pointed out that, unlike the kings that would thereafter rule Israel, he had never taken anything unjustly from his people. He had never oppressed them, as their kings soon would do. He called to mind God's wonderful dealings with Israel (1 Samuel 12:6-11). Yet, in spite of the lessons of the past which they surely should have known, they now sought protection by politics rather than penitence.

Samuel pointed out that a king would make no real difference. The same immutable truth of the past would operate in the future. "If you will fear the Lord and serve Him, and listen to His voice and not rebel against the command of the Lord, then both you and also the king who reigns over you will follow the Lord your God. And if you will not listen to the voice of the Lord, but rebel against the command of the Lord, then the hand of the Lord will be against you, as it was against your fathers" (1 Samuel 12:14, 15).

Just to drive home this point that sounded so much like the preaching of Moses, God did a wonder in their midst. At the call of Samuel, God sent thunder and rain that day. To us that may not seem to be a great wonder, but to the Hebrews who knew that during the time of the wheat harvest in Israel it absolutely never rained, it was a pretty effective attention-getter.

Samuel reminded the people of the faithfulness of God; he promised his continued prayers on their behalf, though they would no longer look to him for primary leadership; and he spoke that truth that should be burned into the consciousness of all God's people: "Only fear the Lord and serve Him in truth with all your heart; for consider what great things He has done for you. But if you still do wickedly, both you and your king shall be swept away" (1 Samuel 12:24, 25).

What do we rely on for the solution of our national and personal problems? Samuel knew that no solution could be effective if it was not grounded in the person, the will, and the revelation of God. Do we?

Timeless Truths

- God hears the deep longings of the committed.
- Hannah gave her first son to God and was blessed with numerous other children (1 Samuel 2:20, 21). God seems to replace with abundance what we give with love.
- "For not by might shall a man prevail" (1 Samuel 2:9).
- Though God did not wish for Israel to have a king, He nevertheless allowed it. God does not always force His will on history.
- God does not abandon man for his bad choices. Rather He uses the harmful results of those choices as a means of teaching His truths.
- Like the Hebrews, Christians sometimes fail to appreciate their special relationship with God and foolishly long for the ways of the world.

13

The Wonder of God's Revelation

(God and His People)

Lesson Text: Psalm 105
Suggested Reading: Psalm 78; Nehemiah 9

"But his delight is in the law of the Lord, and in His law he meditates day and night" (Psalm 1:2).

"On the glorious splendor of Thy majesty, and on Thy wonderful works, I will meditate" (Psalm 145:5).

They were formative years, those often troubled and chaotic years of struggle to become a nation set apart unto God. They were sad years, those years of wandering and dejection that were God's schoolmaster for Israel. They were trusting years, those years of receiving blessing from heaven in both a physical and spiritual sense. They were triumphant years, those years of heady victories against overwhelming odds, those years of collective success in spite of individual conflicts. They were suffering, hoping, believing, failing, disobeying, repenting, conquering, learning years in which Israel was pommeled in God's crucible to become a people uniquely set aside to Him, a people uniquely chosen as the bearer of His revelation.

Our studies began in weakness in a land of bondage; they end in power in a land of promise. We have followed the tortuous and sometimes painful, yet always instructive and exciting, history of the fulfillment of God's promise to Abraham and the establishment of a great nation under God.

A People Honoring His Name

God did wonderful things in the life of this nation. He demonstrated His power in the lives of faithful men and women whom He called and led. He performed great wonders and miracles that demonstrated incontestably that He was indeed the only true God and that His word ought to be regarded as the only standard for truth and conduct. He punished them, when necessary, surely and truly, lest the infection of sin corrupt His special people. He molded a people designed to be sensitive to Him, in tune with Him, and activated by Him and His word. He gave this people laws to regulate their lives and bring sin to their consciousness. He used this people to bring righteous judgment upon the idolatry and wickedness of their enemies, and He used their enemies to chasten and teach them. He raised up judges to bring justice in the land and reformers to bring repentance in the heart. He used military victories to teach them the power of moral purity and military defeats to teach them to search their ways. He prepared a people unto His name, unique in all history.

A History Revealing His Truths

History can be written from a number of different points of view. It can be a mere chronological framework of events. Or it can trace ideas and principles as they shape national consciousness. The history of Israel relates actual events that truly happened, and yet it is primarily moral history. The chroniclers were more eager for their readers to learn lasting truths from the recorded events than for them to learn the events for their own sake.

The history of Israel cumulatively illustrates the truth delivered and reiterated by God's spokesmen, leaders, seers, deliverers, judges, prophets, priests, and angels from the very beginning of the journey to nationhood. Here is the core of that truth: If God's people are to prosper, they must fear the Lord, serve Him in truth with all their heart, and obey His commandments. If they fail to do this, oppression, sorrow, trouble, and pain are inevitable. The positive side of this truth was well put by Moses in the book of Deuteronomy: "And now, Israel, what does the Lord your God require from you, but to fear the Lord your God, to walk in all His ways and love Him, and to serve the Lord your God with all your heart and with all your soul, and to keep the Lord's commandments and His statutes which I am commanding you today for your good?" (Deuteronomy 10:12, 13).

A Remembrance Recalling His Deeds

Important to the impressing of this truth on the consciousness of the people in Israel was the constant reiteration of the wonders of God's dealings with them in their glorious past. Their apostasy was frequently heralded by the notation that they forgot the wonders and miracles that God had performed in their midst. God worked in history. Memory was given to man not just for man's convenience in coping with his environment. It was a gift designed to help him build his life on the proved nature of God as learned and experienced by his forefathers. The great deeds of God were to be remembered through place names and through monuments raised throughout the land. They were brought to mind through special feast days and national holidays like Passover. The events of the past were to be talked of in the home and read in the solemn assemblies. They were recorded in a book to be preserved and constantly referred to (Exodus 17:14; 24:4, 7; Deuteronomy 17:18-20; 28:58-61; 30:9, 10; 31:24-26; Joshua 1:8; 8:31, 34; 23:6; 24:26; 1 Samuel 10:25). God's leading came first to Israel through direct revelation, but that revelation continued to exert influence on the future through written truth, the Bible. How fortunate we are that the great deeds of God were systematically recorded in writing to be handed down to future generations! It is this record that we study as we read the Scriptures.

A Purpose Revealing His Love

It is clear that God was preparing Israel for something special. She was to be an instrument of salvation for all nations, for through her would come God's clearest revelation of himself in Christ Jesus. That, of course, was the greatest wonder ever to be performed in the midst of Israel and in the midst of the world. Isaiah wrote of Jesus, "And His name will be called Wonderful, Counselor, Mighty God, Eternal Father, Prince of Peace" (Isaiah 9:6). And Peter was to proclaim, "Jesus the Nazarene, a man attested to you by God with miracles and wonders and signs which God performed through Him in your midst, just as you yourselves know—this Man, delivered up by the predetermined plan and foreknowledge of God, you nailed to a cross by the hands of godless men and put Him to death" (Acts 2:22, 23).

Blood sacrifice played a great part in the religious life of the Hebrews as they moved toward Canaan. It was the blood of the lamb that marked the houses of the faithful on the night when death swept through Egypt to claim the firstborn. It was blood that was sprinkled on the people as they dedicated themselves to carrying out the commands of God (Exodus 24:8), and it was blood that was shed on the altar of the tabernacle. These things were looking forward to the offering of the perfect sacrifice in Jesus. "In Him," Paul wrote, "we have redemption through His blood, the forgiveness of our trespasses, according to the riches of His grace" (Ephesians 1:7). And the writer to the Hebrews noted, "For if the blood of goats and bulls and the ashes of a heifer sprinkling those who have been defiled, sanctify for the cleansing of the flesh, how much more will the blood of Christ, who through the eternal Spirit offered Himself without blemish to God, cleanse your conscience from dead works to serve the living God?" (Hebrews 9:13, 14).

It is Jesus, Lord and Messiah, raised from the dead by the power of God, through whose sacrifice of himself we have the certain hope of entering God's promised land of eternal rest and blessing.

Is your life filled with the wonders of God? It cannot be if you have not chosen the path of faithfulness to His will as expressed in the wonderful Word that became flesh and dwelt in the midst of wayward humanity that He might open the way into the very presence of God.

Timeless Truths

• Jehovah is a God of history. He is not an abstract force or a principle of nature. He is personally involved with His creation to the point of participating in human events to bring about His righteous purposes.

• The crowning wonder of God's saving work in history is the incarnation.

• There are ever two paths open to man: the path of disobedience and the path of eternal life.

• What we do has consequences not only for ourselves but for others. Sin in the tent pollutes the whole camp (Joshua 7).

• The way of the wicked shall perish.

• The wonder of the past is of little value if it is not brought to mind for the workings of the present.

• God's people treasure the book of His revelation. Truth is not to be found from within man, but from without, by the revelation of God to man.

• The wonders of God come to those who honor God's name with obedient faith.

- "Let the heart of those who seek the Lord be glad" (Psalm 105:3).
- Our confidence must be in God.
- We must never forget the mighty works of God. Forgetfulness leads to sinfulness.
- It is of little use for us to wonder at the demonstrations of God's power if that wonder does not lead us to bend our rebellious wills to His revealed will.

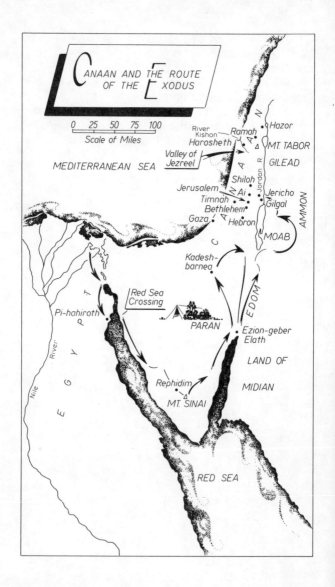

CANAAN AND THE ROUTE OF THE EXODUS

0 25 50 75 100
Scale of Miles

MEDITERRANEAN SEA

River Kishon
Ramah
Hazor
Harosheth
MT. TABOR
Valley of Jezreel
GILEAD
Jordan R.
Shiloh
Jerusalem
Ai
Jericho
Timnah
Gilgal
Bethlehem
Gaza
Hebron
AMMON
MOAB
Kadesh-barnea
Red Sea Crossing
Pi-hahiroth
PARAN
EDOM
Ezion-geber
Elath
LAND OF
Nile River
EGYPT
Rephidim
MIDIAN
MT. SINAI
RED SEA

C A N A A N